WHY FOREIGNERS LIKE HONG KONG

Mark O'Neill

CONTENTS

In the Name of Love

Political Factors

INTRODUCTION

Hong Kong is an international city. According to the 2016 census, eight per cent of its population of 7.34 million were non-Chinese. If you exclude domestic helpers, the percentage was 3.6 per cent, or 264,000 people. Some have been here their entire lives and come from families that settled here generations ago. They have lived here longer than many of the Chinese residents.

This book is a snapshot of the lives of these long-term residents. We aimed for a wide range of races and nationalities, of jobs and sectors, to illustrate the diversity of this foreign presence. It was hard to decide who to include – the choice is too large.

We wish to express our sincere thanks to all the interviewees for giving their precious time and speaking at length about their lives, both in Hong Kong and elsewhere in the world. We sent all of them the draft of the interviews, to revise and correct.

They enrich our society in many ways, such as: the Swiss pastor who counsels those in prison; the Irish priest who has devoted his life to educating secondary school students; the French man who runs two restaurants and imports French craft and organic drinks; the Australian who since 1995 has run a charity that collects unwanted goods and donates them all over the world; the Australian vet who has treated thousands of cats and dogs over the last 25 years; and a Sindhi who runs a foundation that helps ethnic minorities in the city.

We have editions in English and Chinese, excellently translated by Norman Ching. We hope that the book gives the reader an insight and understanding of people he or she has never met before and a deeper knowledge of the rich diversity of Hong Kong.

Chapter. 1

CHILDREN
OF
IMMIGRANTS

1

Born in a POW camp, a True Hongkonger

George Cautherley

George Cautherley was born in the Japanese internment camp in Stanley in September 1942. He is the sixth generation of his family to live in China. His ancestors founded one of the most important early American trading firms in China.

"Hong Kong is where I feel most comfortable," Cautherley said in an interview at the pharmaceuticals company he owns in Chai Wan. "This is where most of my friends and my interests are. To move at my age is very difficult. Hong Kong is my home." George is a true Hong Konger.

His arrival into this world could scarcely have been more dramatic. He was conceived at his parents' home on Mount Austin Road in November 1941. His parents knew it was merely a question of time before the Japanese occupied the city and that they would be interned. "We would need something to focus on during internment," his mother said.

At the time of the surrender, Christmas Day 1941, she was working as a nurse and her husband as an officer in the Hong Kong and Shanghai Bank (HSBC). In January 1942, the couple were taken to the Stanley camp. "When I was due, my mother was suffering from malaria and anemia. There was a typhoon, which delayed my father's arrival by her side. The doctors said that she needed a blood transfusion; she did not have a common blood type. 'Without a transfusion, she will die. With one, she may die,' the doctors said."

Somehow, they found the necessary blood and George was born. He was one of 52 babies born in the camp, between January 1942 and the Japanese surrender in August 1945; he is one of two still living in Hong Kong.

During the internment, his parents were ill much of the time. One rare pleasure was to go to Tweed Bay in Stanley to paddle in the water. "One day I was playing outside. My mother grabbed me and took me inside. I later learned that the Americans had bombed and missed and hit a bungalow not far from where we were."

To feed the infant boy, over the next three and a half years, his mother sold all her jewellery to buy food. HSBC staff outside sent food parcels, including baby food and quality items, to supplement the rations served in the camp. In early 1946, George, three and a half years old, was taken to see a pediatrician in Britain. He said that the boy was very healthy. It was a miracle caused by the love and care of his parents and many others.

Pioneer in China Trade

The history of George's family stretches back to 1801, with the arrival of Daniel Heard, the eldest of his great-great-great uncles in Whampoa with a cargo to trade. On January 1, 1840, Augustine Heard, the youngest of his great-great-great uncles, set up a trading company named after himself in Guangzhou. He was one of several members of the Heard family, from Massachusetts, who went there to expand their business.

For the next 34 years, Augustine Heard & Company was one of the largest American trading companies in the China trade. Helping Augustine was his nephew John Heard – the great-great grandfather of George Cautherley. John arrived in China in 1841, aged 17; by the age of 21, he had earned US$10,000, an enormous sum at that time, and received a 20 per cent equity in the firm.

He stayed in China for 11 years before making his first return to the USA, via Europe. There he met leading citizens, including the Duke of Wellington and author William Makepeace Thackeray.

George's lineage is through his mother's side. The father of his maternal grandmother was Richard Howard Heard, son of John Heard and a Chinese lady. After the trading company went bankrupt, the family went to the U.S. and Europe. In 1880, Richard Heard returned to Hong Kong, to work for Jardine's. In 1882, at the Catholic Cathedral in Caine Road, he married Mary Purcell, daughter of an Irish soldier in the British army; she had been brought up in a Catholic convent in Hong Kong. All their children were born in Hong Kong, including

Cautherley's grandmother.

In 1893, Richard Heard was transferred to Shanghai. He and his wife liked their life there; both died and were buried in Shanghai. In 1912, George's mother, Dorothy, was born in Shanghai; she was one of four children born in the city. To confirm his ancestry, George did DNA tests and put the information on Ancestry platforms on the Internet. From these, he learnt that he is one per cent Chinese and one per cent Spanish and that the children of Roger Lobo are his fourth cousins.

HSBC Marriage Rules

His mother grew up with her siblings in a comfortable home in Shanghai; they had 12 servants. She received her education there and visited Britain only two or three times. In 1931, she was one of the first group of women hired by HSBC in the city; to prove their worth and overcome the prejudice against them, they had to work twice as hard as the men.

Also working in the bank was Joe Cautherley, George's future father. He had moved to Shanghai in 1927, after joining the bank in London. After different postings, he was sent to Hong Kong in 1936. In the same year, Dorothy was evacuated to Hong Kong to work for the bank there from Shanghai to escape an imminent Japanese attack. It was there she met Joe again; the relationship blossomed.

"To marry, a HSBC expatriate officer had to have served 10 years and receive the approval of his superior. If he did not give it and the officer went ahead with the marriage, he had to resign. Before the women chose their dates, they checked on the length of service of potential husbands." In 1938, the two married in St John's Cathedral in Shanghai.

After leave in the UK, Joe was posted to Bombay for a short while and then back to Hong Kong, living on Peak Road, now Mount Austin Road. In 1940, in the expectation of a Japanese attack, the government evacuated the expatriate women and children to Australia. But Dorothy did not want to leave her husband so soon after their marriage. She signed up as a volunteer nurse, an essential service; so she was allowed to stay in Hong Kong. When the hostilities started, HSBC was requested by the Governor to keep the bank operating, so half of its expatriate staff were retained to maintain bank operations, while the other half were released to participate in the defence of Hong Kong; Joe was among the first group. The British Army had mounted guns close to the apartment building where the couple lived. Without a concrete base, the guns had sunk and clipped off the corner of the building. The British Army gave them seven minutes to clear the building, then blew it up. So the couple lost everything.

Parker Pen from a Hong Kong Film Star

After the Japanese surrender on August 15, 1945, George and his parents were released from the camp. They went straight to a transport ship. When they reached the Suez Canal, the Red Cross gave them winter clothes. So, when they arrived in Southampton in southeast England on October 24, 1945, they were warmly dressed. The family went to live with Joe's mother in Royston, near Cambridge.

At the end of October 1946, George's younger brother, Simon, was born. "My father was a dedicated banker and a very loyal person," said George. "He insisted on going back to Hong Kong to work for HSBC. My mother also wanted to return."

In February 1947, the family came back and lived on Waterloo Road. His father was posted to the Kowloon office of the HSBC, in one of the wings of the Peninsula Hotel. "He liked to visit clients and sometimes took me with him," said George. "We went to see tailors and jewellers in Tsim Sha Tsui and factory owners in Tsuen Wan. His policy was to lend to reputable industrialists from Shanghai, even if they had no collateral. He was proved right. The only loan that went bad was to a trader who lost the money gambling. Those in industry

September 2, 1945, George Cautherley and his parents at Stanley. (© George Cautherley)

paid theirs back.

A highlight was a dinner in the large home of a wealthy industrialist on Castle Peak Road. His wife was a film star [Hu Shui-wah] known as 'Butterfly' Wu, who gave me, then a boy of just 11, a Parker 51 pen. That was the height of luxury!"

He attended primary school at Kowloon Junior. In 1951, his father sent George to a boarding school in Sussex in the south of England. It had beautiful grounds and three lakes, where the students ice-skated in the winter. For three consecutive summers, he came to Hong Kong for the holiday; it was a three-day journey by four-engine propeller plane.

In 1955, his father reached retirement age; the bank offered him the chance to manage a small branch in Brunei. So, for three years, Cautherley went there for his summers. In 1960, his parents retired and went to live in the family home in Royston. Since George felt weak academically, he did not go to university. He tried different jobs but liked none of them.

Return to Hong Kong

Then his uncle, in Hong Kong, sent a cable inviting him to join his medical products business. "I did not hesitate. Hong Kong was a nice place. It was time to buckle down." In October 1964, he took a VC-10 and landed at Kai Tak airport, where his uncle met him. "When I felt the spray on my face on the ferry to HK side, I thought: 'I am back home.'"

Born in Shanghai, his uncle had moved to Hong Kong in 1949 and ran two companies, one general trading and the other medical products. George had to learn a new business quickly; he visited hospitals and other customers. "That is the environment of Hong Kong. You learn quickly and make friends. It was a lot of fun." In 1971, he became a managing director of the firm.

His first girlfriend was an English lady; she returned home after six months. After that, all his girlfriends were Chinese. It took four years, helped by his future mother-in-law, to persuade his favourite, Ruby, to accept him.

His father-in-law had grown up in Singapore and moved to Hong Kong. He was an Administrative Officer who worked for the Commissioner of Prisons. George and Ruby married in 1972. George paid for the cocktail reception at the wedding and his father-in-law the Chinese dinner that followed. Their son Julian was born the next year.

Ruby took over the graphic design company of her brother-in-law when he retired. So, with both working, the couple decided to have no more children. In 1979, George's uncle retired and sold his business to Jardine's. Since George did not wish to work for a big corporation, he set up a new company, also in medical products, with a British trading firm; he owned 25 per cent of the equity.

In 1987, he and Ruby paid HK$1.2 million for a 1,500-square-foot

"That is the environment
of Hong Kong. You learn
quickly and make friends. It
was a lot of fun."

apartment in Baguio Villas. In 1991, they went one better – they sold the Baguio apartment and paid HK$7.8 million for an apartment on Mount Kellett Road, with 2,500 square feet and built in 1972. HSBC gave a mortgage to cover 70 per cent of the purchase price.

Their son Julian studied Business Management at City University in London. He returned to Hong Kong and, although he undertook a small project for each of his parents' businesses, which he executed well, he did not find their businesses suited him.

Then he found his vocation was making films. He did internships on film productions in Hong Kong; in 1998, he went to the University of Southern California School of Cinematic Arts. After graduation, he made a short film that won several awards. This enabled him to obtain a "talent" visa that allowed him to remain in the U.S. In 2003, he set up his own film production company; he married an American lady and they are settled in Los Angeles. George's younger brother has lived in Britain since he was eight years old; he has never married.

George has enjoyed a prosperous business life. In 1983, he bought the 75 per cent share he did not already own of the company he was working in. He expanded it. At its peak, it operated two factories, one in Shenzhen and one in Hainan Island, each with 60 employees, and a sales force of over 100 people in China. During the 1990s, his firm sold the highest-selling drug in the Chinese market – "we had 60 imitations," he said.

Over the last 10 years, he has reduced his workload; he comes to work half-time. He sold his business in medical and dental equipment but retained the pharmaceuticals. This part of the business is run by a partner, Daniel Ng, who first joined the firm in 1975 as a young salesman and later returned as sales manager.

In 1993, George spun out his pharmaceutical division into a separate company and gave his sales manager a 50 per cent share. The firm employs over 80 people at its Chai Wan office and factory in Hainan. George is a director in SinoMab BioScience Limited a biotech firm that is listed and has investments in other biotech firms.

George Cautherley and the staff of his Shenzhen factory. (© George Cautherley)

Making Policy

In 1989, George joined the newly founded Hong Kong Democratic Foundation, a bi-lingual political group that later turned into a public policy think tank. In 1992, he was elected vice-chairman and held the post until 2016. He was active in research and drawing up public policy proposals. This enabled him to build up a large network of contacts within the government and professional communities. "I am still involved in public policy, I think there are things I can do," he said.

2 Fifth Generation Descendant of Portuguese and Eurasians with a Passion for Local Heritage and for Club Lusitano

Anthony Correa

Anthony Correa spent 28 years in the financial services industry repairing broken businesses and running other people's money. For three years, he devoted much of his energy to a multi-million-dollar renovation of Club Lusitano, one of the oldest clubs in Hong Kong – it was founded on December 17, 1866.

Sitting in Club Lusitano's stunning, 25th-floor Pastelaria Lusitano overlooking Central and the Chief Executive's residence, he is proud of what they have done. "We wish to celebrate our Portuguese/Macanese identity and our community here that stretches back 500 years in the Pearl River delta. It is unique and long-standing local communities like ours that make Hong Kong different to other cities in China. Hong Kong's multi-cultural diversity is its strength."

Membership is reserved for those with Portuguese nationality and extraction, of whom there are some 200,000 in Hong Kong and Macao. In 1989, Portugal offered full citizenship to those born in Macao before 1981 – a right that Britain did not afford the residents of Hong Kong prior to its handover in 1997.

"We have revitalised the club," said Correa. "We have approximately 400 resident members, between the ages of 18 and 95, of whom 40 per cent are women and another 300 non-resident members. At the lowest point 20 years ago, due to many years of migration we had less than half this number, all men. The club was dying, and we had to make it relevant in the 21st Century.

"Here we can celebrate our unique identity established since Hong Kong's founding in 1842, when Portuguese working for the British East India Company first moved here. We have a very proud history in Hong Kong." says Correa "Most Hong Kong people do not know this, but the first European settlement in the Pearl River delta was established by a Portuguese explorer Jorge Álvares in 1513 called Tamão, modern day Tuen Mun. The Portuguese were there for a few years before being kicked out by the emperor, then a few decades later Macao was born."

In 2019, the opening ceremony of the newly renovated Club Lusitano. (© Anthony Correa)

Deep Roots in China

Correa comes from a family with deep roots in China. They lived for many generations in Macao before his great great grandfather Matias da Luz Soares moved to Hong Kong in the mid-19th century. His great grandfather, Francisco Paulo de Vasconcelos "Frank" Soares, was a real estate developer who was one of the first to develop the Ho Man Tin area in Kowloon. Soares Avenue is named after him, Emma Avenue named after his wife, and Julia Avenue his daughter and Anthony's grandmother. A large Portuguese community lived in Ho Man Tin the first half of the 20th Century.

His father was born in Shanghai and moved to Hong Kong during the anti-Japanese war. He, his brother, and mother lived in the Ho Man

Tin home of Frank Soares during the Japanese Occupation; his uncles were detained in the Sham Shui Po prisoner of war camp because they had joined the Hong Kong Volunteers to fight for Hong Kong and protect their families and homes.

"During the war, my great grandfather Soares was honorary Portuguese consul in Hong Kong. On the day the Japanese invaded Hong Kong, 400 Portuguese civilians from Kowloon and the New Territories came to his house to seek refuge. They did not have time to escape to Macao, as many of the community did and were well aware of the atrocities committed by the Japanese in the Mainland.

"Because they were integrated into society, many of these refugee families had British colonial papers but were considered neutrals by the Japanese due to their Portuguese nationality and heritage. Against the wishes of the Macao Governor where refugees were overwhelming the city, Soares issued them all with Portuguese travel papers so they could escape occupied Hong Kong.

"After that, they all left my great grandfather's home in Liberty Avenue, Ho Man Tin, most fleeing to Macao. But he stayed with my grandmother, my father, and my uncle for the three and a half years of the Occupation. He was the Portuguese consul general, and he had a great sense of duty towards those that remained, including his sons in the POW camp. They almost starved. It was a terrible time for my family, and they lost almost everything during the war."

Correa's father Frank (named after Frank Soares) was educated at La Salle in Kowloon and his grandmother Julia at the nearby Maryknoll Convent School. They were staunch Catholics and attended Sunday Mass at St Teresa's Church in Prince Edward Road. His mother Vivienne, from a long-standing Eurasian family, was also educated in the city; she attended Diocesan Girls School in Jordan, like her mother before her.

The two married in Hong Kong in 1967. In January 1968, like many, they moved to Australia because of the left-wing riots here. So, Correa was born in Sydney in 1968. In 1972, the family returned to

Hong Kong, where his father took over the family business after his father-in-law died.

In 1977, he sold the business and the family moved back to Australia, settling in Melbourne. It was there he attended Xavier College, a Jesuit institution with many Irish-Australian priests, from 1980 to 1985. He grew up in a suburb of Melbourne.

"Fortunately, I and my two brothers were tall and good at sports, especially cricket, basketball, soccer and Australian rules football. We could take care of ourselves and we had a happy childhood in the leafy eastern suburbs of Melbourne. In the 70s there was still a lot of racism down under; local kids often reminded us that we were different to white Australians. In addition to many Aussie good friends, a lot of my friends to this day were from Italian, Greek, Chinese or Vietnamese immigrant families. I retain a strong attachment to the school and head its alumni association here."

In 1986, he entered RMIT University in Melbourne, graduating in 1989 with a degree in Finance. He became a chartered accountant and went to work for Price Waterhouse (PW) in Melbourne.

Return to Hong Kong

In 1992, Correa returned to Hong Kong for the first time in 15 years for a holiday. "I walked into the Club Lusitano to have lunch with then President Arnaldo 'Sonny' de Oliveira Sales and he welcomed me back. He knew my brothers and me as kids from weekends at the Victoria Recreation Club in Sai Kung and Club de Recreio in Jordan."

Correa stayed for three weeks on the roof of his granduncle's house in Waterloo Road and loved it. He took a China Travel Service tour of Guangzhou to get a taste of the Mainland. But he didn't tell his grand-uncle, as it was only three years after Tiananmen Square.

"It was the first time anyone in my family had been to the Mainland since my father left Shanghai as a child. My mother had never been because of fear of communism. After I returned from

In December 1976, Anthony Correa and his family at a festival day of the Club Recreio in Kowloon. (© Anthony Correa)

Guangzhou, my grand-uncle was OK with the trip, but my grand-aunt thought I was crazy to go to the Mainland at that time."

Without an appointment, he went to the office of Price Waterhouse in Prince's Building in Central. He told them that, if they had a vacancy in his department, he would like to apply for it. Then he returned to Melbourne. Six months later, the PW office in Hong Kong contacted him and offered a post in the Corporate Finance and Restructuring department.

"My mother was against my coming. A representative of the United Nations High Commissioner for Refugees in Melbourne, she was proud of her new country and fearful of the unstable Mainland she knew in her childhood. But my father said: 'You have to go and see the world. It will toughen you up and give you great experience.'"

So, Correa took the job and moved in 1993 to Hong Kong, where he has remained ever since.

He rejoined the Portuguese community, reacquainting himself with many of his parents' extended family and friends – more aunties and uncles. He was welcomed back to his first lunch at the Club Lusitano by Jesuit Fr Marciano Baptista. Fr Baptista and his father's families were close for generations in both Hong Kong and Macau. Fr Baptista had also taught at Xavier College in Melbourne for several years, so knew Correa well when he was a teenager.

Correa was very active in sports and joined the Kowloon Cricket Club, captaining teams and playing national level cricket for Hong Kong. He also served as the Honorary Treasurer of the Hong Kong Paralympic Committee and Sports Association for the Physically Disabled.

At PW in Australia, he had worked in corporate finance and restructuring; so, this was the department he joined in Hong Kong and moved quickly up the ranks. Correa continued the work in restructuring as he had done in Melbourne, mainly on behalf of HSBC and Standard Chartered in the lead up to the Asian Financial crisis in 1997. At that time, PW had 500 people in Greater China, including small offices in Guangzhou and Shanghai. "Most everyone knew everyone, so it was a great place to work and get to know people in Hong Kong."

Banks entrusted to PW the restructuring of defaulting companies to cover debts that were unpaid. "We had to find solutions, it was a complex world. We went to Dongguan in Guangdong to wind up factories. At that time, the laws pertaining to creditors' rights were limited, everything had to be negotiated. This sometimes involved closing factories and putting people out of work. Sometimes it got confrontational with employees and suppliers who did not understand. It was difficult to explain why the owners had left and the banks had taken over. We mainly represented the banks and the creditors."

Head of Proprietary Trading

After six years with PW in Hong Kong, he moved in 1998 to Nomura Securities Co., Ltd., Japan's biggest brokerage firm, as head of proprietary trading for Asia. He was just 30 years of age. He stayed with them for five years.

In 2004, he married his wife Rebecca, a Singaporean Chinese lawyer; they held the ceremony in the Yarra Valley in Victoria, Australia. He decided to take a one-year break that included organising their wedding. They now [in 2021] have three children, aged between 8 and 13; they speak both English and Mandarin.

A new form of financial institution was coming into being – the hedge fund. "There are many types of funds but the general idea was that we in the fund partner with the clients in making the investments in special complex situations, distressed or to take advantage of market volatility and inefficiencies."

Correa decided to join one, Polygon Global Partners, in 2005. He and his wife lived for one year in London, where he worked in its office. After one year, he returned to Hong Kong to set up its operations here.

After four years with Polygon, he set up his own hedge fund,

Black's Link Capital in 2009, with six other colleagues from Polygon. The firm was named after a hiking and running trail near the Peak. In 2011, he joined Taconic Capital Advisors LP, where he worked for seven years.

During his nearly three decades in finance, he was involved in many of the best-known restructuring and distressed situations, such as: Peregrine Capital and Noble Group of Hong Kong; Samsung and Hyundai of South Korea; Astra International of Indonesia; Olympus, Elpida and Livedoor of Japan; and Sino-Forest of China.

"It was exciting and challenging work. It could be stressful, involving restructuring that sometimes includes, selling assets, cutting costs and staff. Working with lawyers and other stakeholders meant disputes. You learn a lot about legal systems and the long legal delays in places like India!"

Remaking Club Lusitano

Since 2018, he has devoted much of his energy to the renovation of Club Lusitano. It took two years of planning and 18 months to carry out with the architects and builders; it was completed on time and on budget. He has done the work pro bono, as have many other volunteers in the Portuguese community who have architectural, design, business, finance and legal backgrounds. "The city has been very good to me. Here I met my wife, and we created our family. I wanted to give something back," Correa said.

The clubhouse occupies the top five floors of a 27-storey high-rise on Ice House Street in Central. Below are 20 floors of office space and a three-level ground floor retail podium

A threestorey Cruz de Cristo sits on top of the building; it recalls the early Portuguese ships which carried the distinctive, equalarmed red cross as a symbol of their faith. The grand ballroom, on the 27th floor, is the Salao Nobre de Camoes. It is the most spectacular room in the club. Three sides of double height floor-to-ceiling crenulated windows afford spectacular views of the shining skyscrapers of Hong Kong. They overlook the home and office of the Chief Executive on one side, and the HSBC building on the other.

One wall displays two stanzas from the epic work *Os Lusíadas* by Luís Vaz de Camões, for whom the room is named. Another features a map of the world at the entrance showing the routes taken by the 15th & 16th century pioneering Portuguese explorers and mariners.

In 2003, the club admitted women members for the first time.

"I first joined the general committee in 2002. The club faced an existential crisis. Most other members of the General Committee at that time were in their 80s. They were very old-fashioned Portuguese, but they were grand old men like Sir Albert Rodrigues, Sir Roger Lobo and Comendador Arnaldo "Sonny" Sales. We had to be respectful towards them as they were like "uncles" to us all. Unless the elderly committee members knew them personally at that time, it was very difficult to get in.

"We had to reform the Hong Kong Portuguese identity and open to the wider community in Hong Kong and Macao to be relevant. The new HK-Macao-Zhuhai bridge was opening, so the large Portuguese community in Macao would be a bus ride away."

The club is restricted to those holding Portuguese nationality. Did this mean they had to speak the Portuguese language? A small minority of the 200,000 citizens in Macao and Hong Kong are able to, but the majority have been assimilated into the communities of the two cities and do not speak Portuguese, but Cantonese and English. Today these are the two main languages of the club, but there remains Portuguese spoken by some members and some of the staff.

"We want to retain the Lusophone traditions and have reinitiated Portuguese classes recently that were very popular, as it's still the sixth most spoken language in the world by 260 million people. However, we also need to be practical and localise in Hong Kong, we needed to speak Cantonese and English for our daily lives.

"The renovation needed to reflect our hybrid identity – not

With Tony Blair, when Correa was working at Polygon Global Partners. (© Anthony Correa)

entirely Chinese, nor entirely Portuguese. Now Putonghua will become more important, and our far eastern Portuguese community will adapt. The Portuguese have been in India, Indonesia, Timor, Malaysia, Korea and Japan for hundreds of years and learned all of those languages and cultures too."

Club Lusitano raised the money needed to renovate entirely from within. The renovation process was done openly and transparently with "town hall" meetings, shared design plans and members surveys. They invited the members to make proposals on what should be done.

"Previously, the club was very dreary with old wood panels and a single dining room on the 26th floor. Now we have three, including a coffee shop called Pastelaria and a buffet in the bar. On the 26th floor fine dining restaurant, we have an executive chef and many products from Portugal. We serve both Portuguese and Macanese cuisine as well food influenced by other former far eastern Portuguese cities like

Goanese style curries and Cantonese favorites like chow mein and Hong Kong toast. *Pastel de Nata* are egg tarts made in our Portuguese tradition. Tempura was first brought to Japan by the Portuguese, and we serve our version called *Peixinhos da Horta*."

The new club boasts a mahjong room, a card room, biblioteca/library, and several function rooms, which members can hire for private events. It has one of the largest collections of Portuguese wines and spirits in Asia. There are many artifacts in the club including an aircraft propeller from the first flight from Lisbon to Macau, old bibles in both Portuguese and English and a library with many books including some in Macau patois.

In 2016, the club started a quarterly magazine, which records the many stories of the Portuguese community here. That year it started a website and Facebook Page. And it initiated reciprocal arrangements with former majority Portuguese clubs the Victoria Recreation Club and Club de Recreio.

Correa also serves as an advisor to the Macanese Families website that contains the genealogy of all the Macanese community, "It is a living website which we update regularly. We are a living club. That is the legacy we want to leave for the next generation."

"My advice to the other communities in Hong Kong is to keep them relevant and be proud of their history."

Arc of History

Correa said that he and his wife made a conscious decision to ensure that their three children could speak, read, and write bilingually, English and Mandarin, so that they can live and work in Greater China if they wish.

One of his two brothers has also lived and worked in Hong Kong and Singapore, spending a good part of his career in Asia. His sister lived and worked for over six years in Beijing and speaks Mandarin. "In some ways, it's not too different to the Portuguese community in my father's and grandfather's time. We know Asia and the China Coast well and moved to where the trade, work and economic opportunity was. Nowadays it's called globalisation and the Portuguese Community understand this better than most after trading for five centuries in Asia."

The Correas chose for their son and eldest daughter the private Chinese International School in Braemar Hill. "Students in year 10 spend a year at a school in the Mainland. Our daughter is in Hangzhou for a year starting this August. All schools in Hong Kong should do this. It is the future. The more experience children have of China, the better. Our daughter is even thinking of studying in the Mainland for part of her undergraduate studies as one of her tertiary options."

Correa said that, in the past, the consensus was that there were better opportunities in the West, but this had changed. "The arc of history is in favour of Asia now. We are returning to the pre-colonial era. The West has become more inward-looking, except perhaps for parts of Europe like Germany. Trump, Marine Le Pen, and Brexit are extreme examples of this, but in Hong Kong and Macao we know globalisation benefits both East and West and has created huge prosperity for hundreds of years."

"No-one imagined how China would change from North Korea to California in two generations. How was it possible? It has dealt very competently with Covid-19. It will be a bumpy road, but I am optimistic."

"This city has been very good to me. It was here
I met my wife and we have made our family
here. I want to give something back."

3 Building a Family
Empire in Service
Apartments and Fiji
Resort

Pilar Morais

Pilar Morais runs a chain of five-star service apartments in Hong Kong and a resort in Fiji. She is also the mother of three children, a keen sportswoman and active in school and community affairs. Her life is overflowing.

Her company is CHI International, a business she founded in 2007 with her father Philip and two brothers. Philip belongs to a seventh-generation Macanese family. His parents moved to Hong Kong after World War Two, to give their children better opportunities.

Philip has been Pilar's role model. In 2021 he was 73, chairman of the company and still playing an active role.

The Covid pandemic has been a disaster, as for all firms in the hotel and hospitality industry. "Our current occupancy rate is 30 per cent," Pilar said. "The normal is 85-90 per cent. In the current climate, 30 per cent is good."

Close Ties at King George V School

She was born on May 22, 1982 in San Francisco. Her mother chose to give birth to her and her two brothers in the United States, so that they would be U.S. citizens and have more opportunities.

Raised and educated in Hong Kong, she attended the English Schools Foundation's primary and secondary schools, Kowloon Junior School and King George V School (KGV).

Among the Macanese, her parents were unusual. After the leftist riots during the 1960s, a majority of this community, holding Portuguese passports, decided to emigrate, to the United States, Canada, Australia, Brazil and Europe.

Most of my family went to the east coast of Australia and to California and one went to Denmark," said Pilar. "But my father had confidence in Hong Kong. He always had and still has today."

Her father came from a humble background. He lived with his family in a small apartment in Hillwood Road with five other Macanese families, a total of 20 people. They installed a "false" floor across the main room; the children slept above and the adults below. He attended Portuguese Community Schools, Inc., Escola Camões, La Salle College and Hong Kong Polytechnic.

He started his career with HSBC. He later worked at a Canadian investments company and then a Swiss company, where he focused on mutual funds. In 1975, he bought his first property and formed his own company. By the 1980s, he had a diversified portfolio of properties.

An entrepreneur, he obtained the Hong Kong franchise for Chuck E. Cheese and Burger King; but it was hard to compete against the power and reach of McDonald's.

So, he set up his own brand of children's indoor entertainment, The Wonderful World of Whimsy , with video games, bowling and other items. It became the market leader in the city. Philip opened a total of 37 stores. It was financially risky – he leased the properties and did not own them.

Then he moved into a new sector – service apartments. During a summer visit to London, he visited such an apartment in Eccleston Place; he saw that such a product had a place in Hong Kong, offering short-term accommodation to business people who wanted an alternative to a hotel. It provided more space and independence, for a similar price.

So, back in Hong Kong, in 1991, he bought a building, paying 10 per cent and borrowing the rest. He renovated it into service apartments on each floor. It was the first such facility in the city and the start of a business which has sustained the family ever since. A year later, he sold the building for a profit of over 100 per cent.

This convinced him to invest more in this sector. He formed his own brand Shama and built a total of 250 service apartments across the city. He bought an office building opposite Times Square and converted it into apartments. In 1991, he bought six floors of the office building in Wyndham Street in which CHI has its office today.

Pilar and her two brothers knew their father's business very well. "He used to take us as children to his meetings. He wanted to involve

Pilar's father and grandmother. (© Pilar Morais)

us in what he was doing."

She greatly enjoyed her education at KGV junior and senior schools. She chose to specialise in computer science, business, maths and psychology. She excelled at sports, representing Hong Kong at hockey and tennis, and was also selected for its netball team.

"It had a strong sense of community. The bridesmaids at my wedding were all classmates from KGV. My best friends today are also my classmates." She maintains her connection with the school by chairing its finance committee and involvement in alumni relations.

In 1991, Samantha Martin, a family friend, founded the Kely Support Group, a charity for young people. Initially it helped those with drug or alcohol problems; since, it has spread to mental health and well-being and positive youth development. Celebrating its 30th year in 2021, it is active in over 90 local and international schools, offering services in Chinese and English. Pilar is on the board and chairs the Fundraising & Events Committee and the 30th Anniversary Committee.

Los Angeles – Too Much Driving, Not Enough Security

For university, Pilar chose the Marshall School of Business at the University of Southern California (USC) in Los Angeles. She also applied to universities in Britain, including King's College, London. "When I went to campuses in the UK, they did not know how to deal with me. There was no welcome. But, at USC, there were open arms and a particular professor showing me all it had to offer."

She studied Corporate Finance. She played a lot of hockey and netball, mostly with British, Australian and New Zealand friends; these are not games popular with Americans. She stayed three and a half years. "I did not like Los Angeles. The city is sprawling and you need to spend a lot of time in the car. Coming from Hong Kong, walking around in the evening was dangerous for young girls. My extended family was in San Francisco, in northern California."

In January 2004, she moved to Sydney, Australia. "I wanted another experience. My parents put no pressure on me to come home or join the family business." But the experience did not turn out well. She was unemployed for two months; companies did not want to hire someone who did not fit their traditional profile. She was not white nor male and did not have a degree from an Australian university.

In March, she was finally hired by a boutique finance company; she stayed there for three and a half years. After work, she would go for a surf, then head home to walk the dogs, then home for dinner.

There she was struck by a chronic disease, ulcerative colitis, that leads to inflammation and ulcers of the colon and rectum. She worked from home. Her meals were prepared by her then boyfriend. For two weeks, she was bed-ridden.

As chairperson of the finance committee of King George V School, Pilar has been active in the alumni association. She has kept close relations with her alma mater. (© Pilar Morais)

Her parents came to visit. "Mother said: 'what are you doing here?' The Australian lifestyle is the kind you should have when you retire. At your age, you should work hard and play hard. Come back to Hong Kong. She was right. It was an easy decision to take." In July 2007, she returned to Hong Kong. She finished her uncompleted projects for the Sydney finance company remotely.

Founding CHI

After selling Shama in 2006, Philip had made enough money to retire. But that was not his nature; he needed to be active, and property was his favoured field. He had found that the annual return from service apartments was nine per cent, compared to six per cent from hotels.

So Philip and his children set up a new company, CHI International, and returned to the business of service apartments. They bought their first building at 279 Shanghai Street, in Kowloon, and converted it. In 2007, they bought three more properties, also in Kowloon, and converted them.

In the summer of 2008, they opened the first three. Then the Asian financial crisis struck – and they lost their core clients – white male investment bankers in their 20s and 30s.

"We had an occupancy rate of only 20 per cent," said Pilar. "We had to change strategy and attract other clients." These included mainland women who had come to Hong Kong to give birth and executives in the garment industry, including mainland Chinese, Indians and Japanese.

"We had to make changes. Initially, the apartments were smoke-free. But the new clients didn't quite grasp that and would continue to smoke, stubbing their cigarettes out in cups."

As of 2021, the company had four properties in Hong Kong, with over 200 apartments. Its market niche is affordable high-end, competing with five-star hotels. It describes them as "balanced living spaces perfectly suited to provide guests with the comfort of a true home away from home. The residences combine thoughtful interior design with the latest facilities and friendly service, connecting you to your destination whilst offering a retreat in which you can relax and unwind."

The sizes range from 290 to 2,400 square feet and prices from HK$17,600 to HK$150,000 a month. The one in Sai Ying Pun, with 19 units, is open to pets, including dogs, cats and tortoises.

They must design interiors to suit a range of clients and tastes. "We choose décor that is neutral and timeless. We use the work of Hong Kong artists," she said.

The market is competitive. CHI is competing not only against other service apartments but also the many four- and five-star hotels trying to attract the same clientele for short-term stays.

"Hong Kong will be our base. We will maintain the same business. We are looking at Portugal and London. The world will be more connected."

Resort in Fiji, Failed in Shanghai

For six years, the firm invested in Shanghai. It converted a 1950s cinema into a 49-room hotel; but it never opened.

It obtained management contracts for three buildings with service apartments. They employed as general manager a Shanghai-born man who had been educated at Cornell and worked with Philip in the United States. The buildings were profitable.

But, to their chagrin, they discovered that the general manager had betrayed them by signing a separate contact with the developer who owned the buildings. "He cut us out. Our 25 years of working with him counted for nothing. We lost a ton of money."

The firm also looked at projects in Thailand and New Zealand but decided not to proceed.

One that went ahead was the Garden Island Resort on Taveuni, the third largest island in Fiji. It is a 90-minute flight by propeller plane from the country's Nadi International Airport. "The resort, with 30 rooms, offers panoramic ocean views, breathtaking sunsets, golf, tennis, sea fishing, diving and bird watching," according to the company.

This project is a result of Philip's 42-year connection with Fiji. When he was 25, Gammon hired him to sell properties in Fiji to expatriates in Hong Kong. Philip himself bought the largest house on the estate. From 2004, the family began to stay there more often. Then they bought the oldest and largest hotel on Taveuni and turned it into the resort. "We are avid divers. We have a personal connection to the place from going there for many years," she said. Pilar's brothers are responsible for marketing it.

Family

In 2011, Pilar married her former classmate, a software engineer and investor. They have three children – nine, seven and one. They live in Clearwater Bay. The two elder children attend Harrow, but will

Pilar and her family. (© Pilar Morais)

move to KGV and complete their studies, like their parents.

Outside the service apartments, she has opened a neighbourhood café, Opendoor Cafe and Courtyard, and an event space, PLATFORM, in Sai Ying Poon.

Philip has based himself in the Philippines but is by no means retired. He has needed four operations on his back.

What of the future? "Hong Kong will be our base. We will maintain the same business. We are looking at Portugal and London. The world will be more connected."

Pilar has British, Australian and Portuguese passports, giving her ease of travel around the world. Her children also have U.S. passports.

She and her brothers gave up their American passports because of the stringent reporting requirements implemented by its government after the 2008 financial crisis. "These obligations are very troublesome. Coutts Bank cut off our relationship after 35 years. I had a three-hour interview with them, but that was not sufficient to satisfy their requirements."

4 HK-born and Raised Indian Woman Pioneer in Law and Investment

Ferheen Mahomed

Ferheen Mahomed has devoted her professional life to Hong Kong, working as a top legal adviser to two French banks and the city's stock market regulator.

But she cannot obtain an SAR passport and fears that the city is losing its drive and ambition.

"People are not as hungry as before," she said. "They are more complacent. I am concerned about Hong Kong, that it is losing its mojo. It does not have the 'get up and go spirit' it used to. Parents mollycoddle their children and do not necessarily allow them to spread their wings and make mistakes, which is very much the pre-requisite to success."

For her dozens of business trips to the Mainland, she used a visa in her BNO passport, but, since 2021, the BNO is no longer recognised by China since the United Kingdom announced that BNO passport holders could apply for residency in the UK and eventually get citizenship. Ferheen has no intention of applying for residency in the UK; being denied the recognition of the BNO passport effectively removes her ability to travel to the Mainland. She is of the view that the non-recognition of the BNO passport should only apply to those who have applied for residency in the UK and not all and sundry.

Applying for an SAR passport is not straightforward for a non-Chinese as one needs to be naturalised. While Ferheen is willing and able to be naturalised, it appears that this is a discretion that the immigration department needs to exercise in her favour.

Fighting Poverty

Ferheen was born in Hong Kong on May 24, 1965 into a modest Muslim Indian family. Her father, who was born in Macao, was the fourth generation of his family to live in South China. Each of them had returned to India to find a wife through an arranged marriage. Her mother was born in the Dadar district of Mumbai, formerly known as Bombay.

She was the second child; her elder sister was born in Macao. Her father moved to Hong Kong and ran his own import/export business. It did not go smoothly and the family was not well-to-do.

Her mother did not go out to work because she considered this would harm the family's status and the daughters' marriage prospects. However, to make ends meet, she became a seamstress, working from home and making the clothes worn by Muslim women.

"My mum's sewing, knitting and embroidery was exquisite. I still have the sweaters she knitted for me and have framed up some of her amazing embroidery pieces. It is art in its purest form," says Ferheen of her mother's work.

Ferheen went to a local primary school, Sacred Heart Canossian, where she learnt Cantonese and made Chinese friends. "I was the only brown girl. All my friends were local. I surely looked different and acceptance was an issue. I was determined to be accepted and I totally assimilated into the Chinese culture, studying Chinese, eating Chinese food, speaking only in Cantonese, watching Cantonese films and even playing mah-jong."

At home, her mother spoke to her in Hindi and she replied in Cantonese.

For her secondary school, she remained at Sacred Heart, a Catholic establishment. "I went to church every day and was impressed by the religion. My mother was a devout Muslim. I did not study Arabic or know the Quran at all. She would have preferred to send me to Island School, but we could not afford it. By that time, I had totally assimilated into the school and was grateful for the opportunity to remain at Sacred Heart. To this day, my close group of friends are from Sacred Heart. There is no cultural or racial gap amongst us. As my friends say, I am more Chinese than the Chinese."

Her aim was to escape the net of poverty in which many of the lower-income South Asians were trapped. "At 11, I decided to become a lawyer. I was inspired by Perry Mason [an attorney in a popular US television series]. I wanted to be a litigator, like Mason. I was active in the debating society, in school and university."

She applied for and won a scholarship to study law at Oxford University, which was a dream come true for Ferheen. Sadly, however, the scholarship only covered the course and flight but not the living expenses. While she tried to obtain sponsorships, it was not meant to be.

Luckily, she had also won a place to study law at Hong Kong University (HKU). She strived hard at HKU and joined the Philip C. Jessup International Law Moot Court Competitions, which is effectively legal debating, and together with the team brought HKU to the top four in the world. She and the Jessup team remain close and meet almost every quarter. To this date, they are called the Jessup Follies, a term coined when they foolishly decided to hold an auction to raise money to get them to compete internationally since the Law School did not have funding at the time. It was an amazing success with the students and lecturers participating with gusto and helping the teams to raise funds so that they could travel and participate.

During the summer, she worked as an intern in the Hong Kong office of Baker & McKenzie, one of the world's largest law firms. "It was a very good international programme, taking students from Hong Kong and overseas, which allowed for a dynamic and international exchange of ideas. We also worked hard and played hard."

During Ferheen's third year at HKU, her mother was watching television while stitching at home and heard about the Rhodes Scholarship. She learnt that the Rhodes Trust was offering one fellowship per year at Oxford University to a Hong Kong student. It was the third year such an offer was made in Hong Kong. The fellowship was very generous, covering tuition, accommodation, flights and living expenses. No shortfall this time!

Ferheen applied and was selected for the final group of applicants. They were invited to an interview at HKU by a panel of eight, including Henry Litton, a prominent lawyer and judge. It was an intimidating experience for the young students.

Then it was down to a short list of four, including three Hong Kong Chinese. They were put into a discussion group for two sessions, as the judges watched on. The panel interview and group discussion were a whole-day affair, extremely nerve-wracking, and lasted from 09:00 to 17:00, with a lunch break. Ferheen was over the moon to be selected. To this day she counts her lucky stars and attributes it to her mother's awareness of the scholarship and her encouragement of Ferheen to apply.

"No White Boy"

Her mother was delighted at her success but also apprehensive at her going to England for two years. She told her not to have a white boyfriend or sex before marriage.

Since Ferheen had never seen her maternal grandmother, she decided to spend a month in India en route for Britain. She stayed in Mumbai, Bangalore and Goa, visiting members of her family.

"My mother was a good storyteller. She prepared me well for the visit. She described the house where she had been born. From her, I had a sense of the vision, smells and taste of India. So it was no shock. In addition, I could speak Hindi. Grandmother was thin and petite and very progressive. She kissed me on the head and said: 'Go and see the world, child, and do what you want.'"

Other members of the family had a different opinion. They were proud that she had been accepted as a Rhodes scholar but said that she did not need to go to Britain. Having won this status, she should stay in India and use it to find an appropriate husband. Little did they know that no one was keen to marry a headstrong girl who was rather wild.

She spent her first year at St John's College, the first Hong Kong person to study there. "It had the best law library, the best grounds, inspirational tutors and fellow students. The food was exceptional as well. My mentor Leo Goodstadt studied at St John's and knew I would be inspired there."

She spent her second year in a house shared with four students of theoretical physics, from Germany, Mexico, Canada and England. It was truly inspirational to be with people outside her own discipline and comfort zone. It was almost like learning a new language.

Her thesis was on "Recognition of Foreign Judgements" for which she received an A grade. Her housemates were instrumental in helping her achieve the grade, as their comments were gruelling. "Physicists are extremely logical and challenge every assumption. It taught me to see the law from a different perspective." Ferheen said she is fated to be connected to physicists as her elder son is studying physics at Imperial College London.

During her studies in Oxford, partners from Baker & McKenzie in Hong Kong would visit her during visits to Britain. They said she was gregarious and suited to working in a firm and with a team. While she had always wanted to be a barrister, she saw there was some truth in their analysis of her personality, coupled with the fact that a solicitor enjoyed a good, fixed salary, while a barrister was self-employed.

This high-level lobbying persuaded her to return to Hong Kong, in 1990, to train as a solicitor with Baker & McKenzie. After she qualified, she joined Slaughter & May in Hong Kong and moved to the City of London with them from 1994 to 1996.

Love Life

It was in Hong Kong in 1992 that she met a Malaysian boy, her future husband. A Malaysian Chinese, he was working in the city for six months. Their courtship was primarily long-distance – with no WhatsApp text messages or WhatsApp calls. He worked in London when they met. He then moved to Hong Kong for her and, shortly thereafter, she moved to London. She then moved back to Hong Kong and he decided to move to the UK to pursue an MBA. He then moved to Malaysia and she moved to Singapore.

After almost six years of courtship, they decided to wed, while still living in different countries. They won over both sides of the family and surmounted racial, cultural and religious challenges.

On the day of the wedding, the boy had to travel down from Malaysia to Singapore, where she was living, to have the ceremony. A weekend celebration at Langkawi (in Malaysia) ensued, which is fondly remembered by their friends and family until now. It was extremely chill and casual, with the groom and his friends getting back late for the wedding dinner as they were playing golf at Datai and the game kept being interrupted by thunderstorms!

They only finally decided on Hong Kong as their home a few months after the wedding! It has been home since they moved back in 1998.

The couple's first son, Joe, was born on March 16, 1999. The second, Chris, was born on December 12, 2003. Joe went to study physics at Imperial College in London and Chris attended an English school in Malaysia. They speak Cantonese, Mandarin and English. At home, Ferheen and her husband speak Cantonese and English.

Career

Marriage and children did not keep Ferheen from pursuing her career; her husband and children always supported her in that – potential tiger mums should be fiercely encouraged to spend their energies outside the family.

Ferheen became General Counsel for the Asia Pacific region and member of the Global Law Steering Committee of the French bank Societe Generale. She was with the bank for almost 13 years.

The job was exhilarating. Her area of responsibility extended from Japan to India and the Philippines; she had to familiarise herself with the legal systems and peculiarities of conducting business in these countries.

The bank at that time was developing its derivatives platforms and derivative products in the region. This was a challenge as the bank was

"You never know where you are.
Chaos is daily. I thrived in it. Every
day I was outside my comfort zone."

a pioneer in many of these products and it was important to navigate the regulatory landscape carefully.

"I was always flying. I hardly took time off for the children. My husband was far better with the children, especially when they were young. He is a devoted father and the best husband who has always given me the freedom I need, a totally selfless and beautiful person."

In June 2010, she moved to brokerage and investment group CLSA for a bigger role as Global General Counsel, thereby giving it exposure beyond Asia and covering the UK, US and Europe. She was also a member of its Global Executive Committee. Her travelling became even more gruelling, to countries as far as the Netherlands, Britain and the US.

One of her significant achievements at CLSA was the negotiation and sale of CLSA to CITIC, a conglomerate owned by the Chinese government. This involved obtaining regulatory approvals in 22 countries.

In June 2014, she became Executive Vice President, Business Development, of the Pacific Century Group (PCG). Founded in Hong Kong in 1993, this is a conglomerate having interests in telecoms, media, internet solutions, property development, asset management and insurance.

"This was the most challenging job as it required more than legal skills. Financing and business acumen were key in driving deals and resolving issues."

She dealt with many issues – regulatory, acquisitions, financing and the media. There was also much travel, to the United Kingdom, Europe and the Middle East.

"You never know where you are. Chaos is daily. I thrived in it. Every day I was outside my comfort zone."

She was then head-hunted to join The Stock Exchange of Hong Kong Limited as Group General Counsel at the Hong Kong Exchanges and Clearing Company, reporting to Charles Li and being a member of the management committee.

She was instrumental in all acquisitions by HKEX and strategic development and Fintech initiatives, including the connect schemes, stock and bond connect, development of derivative products, including the MCSI future contracts.

She held the job for nearly four years, until the end of 2020. "I loved it. I am glad I did it. It gave me a good insight on the interactions between buy side, sell side, regulators and Hong Kong Inc and allowed me to contribute to the development of Hong Kong's capital and financial market through the projects I worked on. It was also an amazing opportunity to work with Charles who is razor sharp and gets things done."

She decided to leave when Li left (at the end of 2020) as she always wanted to strike out on her own and experience what that would be like.

At the beginning of 2021, she set up her own company, C & TM Limited, a corporate and transaction management company offering execution services in mergers and acquisitions, listings and advisory services, especially in crisis situations.

"Through my extensive network of contacts globally both from my general counsel roles and Rhodes Scholar network, I am able to help clients identify and assemble the right teams of advisers and provide a co-ordinated and targeted execution," she declares on her website.

"I am working even harder than before. I am the sole employee of my firm. My model is to work with the client and their teams and their advisers."

Anxious over Hong Kong's Future

She is concerned about the future of Hong Kong. "The wealth gap is getting bigger and this issue needs to be resolved with a sense of urgency. Social and economic imbalances affect the stability of Hong Kong."

She believes that, to remain competitive, Hong Kong also needs to welcome people with global talents and experience. As a global city, Hong Kong needs to maintain its international appeal and competitiveness.

5   Member of a Sindhi Business Family

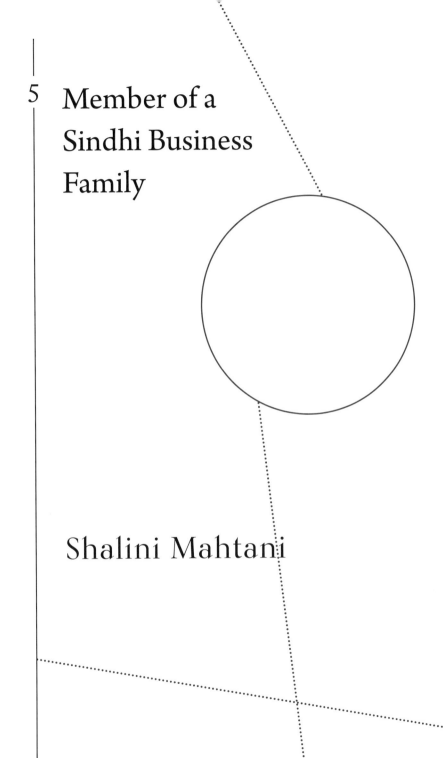

Shalini Mahtani

Shalini Mahtani is founder of the Zubin Mahtani Gidumal Foundation, which she set up in 2014 with her husband Ravi Gidumal, in memory of her beloved son Zubin. He died in May 2009 at the age of three from medical negligence. The Foundation works to improve the lives of the ethnic minorities of Hong Kong.

According to the 2016 census, eight per cent of the city's 7.34 million people – 584,000 – were not ethnic Chinese. The largest group, about 348,000, were from Indonesia, Thailand and the Philippines, most of them domestic maids. The second largest group were 80,000 South Asians from India, Pakistan, Nepal, Bangladesh and Sri Lanka. It is this second group whom the Foundation aims to help.

Growing up in a Conservative, Hindu Family

Mahtani was born in Hong Kong in April 1972 into a conservative Hindu business family from the Sindhi community. Her mother was born in Hong Kong and her father came to Hong Kong at the age of five. Her father studied at Raimondi College and her mother at King George V School. Her mother was the daughter of George Harilela, the older brother of Hari, who was often dubbed the richest Indian in Hong Kong.

"Trading is the main source of income for Sindhis," said Mahtani. "We are like the Jews, with great networks around the world and adaptability. We lost our homeland."

Under the *Partition of India* in 1947, the British awarded the entire province of Sindh to Pakistan; the large majority of its Hindu population left.

Mahtani lived in the family home in Stubbs Road and attended schools of the English Schools Foundation.

"Mine was a conservative family and the main purpose of a girl was to become a good wife. Anything else was considered irrelevant and education not considered a priority." For a husband, it was made clear to her that she would have to choose a member of the Sindhi community.

"To escape my predicament, I wanted to obtain an education and go to university, so I could create my own future. I studied all I could between the ages of 13 and 18 and went from being an average student to a good student.

"I was determined to not live the life of my cousins, marry young and become the object of a man. They seemed happy but I knew that I could not be in the same situation. I found the prevailing view of women in my community unacceptable. I felt like chattel, owned first by my father and then in the future by a husband.

"I went to Island School, which was a very white school at that time. It did not celebrate diversity; we all had to conform to a 'White Anglo-Saxon Way'. My best friends were mostly Asians and Eurasians. In a history lesson, when I was 13, I gave a correct answer to a question which other students had answered wrongly. The teacher commented: 'You might be smart but, in the end, it will count for nothing. Like many other Indian women, you will just be married off.' He did not encourage me but rather dampened my enthusiasm."

Finally, however, her parents permitted her to study in university, thanks to her own excellent academic record and the encouragement of the deputy headmaster of Island School; he said that she was one of the brightest students he had ever taught. But her parents only allowed her to study in London, where members of the Sindhi community could "keep an eye on her". They also forbade her from studying law, her subject of choice, saying that it would make her more difficult and argumentative and ultimately their view was that "Indian men do not want a wife who is too smart!". She would study economics.

When she was 13, she went to India for the first time, with her parents to attend the wedding of a cousin in Bombay, now Mumbai. "Our flight arrived in the middle of the night and we reached the apartment building of my aunt. When we walked out of the lift at her floor, the corridor was pitch black. I was stepping on something. I became frightened. My parents told me just to follow their voice."

After reaching her aunt's apartment and switching on the light, she discovered that she had been walking on people and their blankets. The domestic helpers of her aunt slept in the corridor. "I was appalled by this. I could not get over it."

The next morning, the women put on their beautiful clothes and best jewellery for the wedding at one of the city's most famous hotels. When their car stopped in traffic, people banged on the windows; one was a girl with bare breasts, feeding a baby. "I tried to wind down the window but was told not to, for fear we would be mobbed. I did not understand this." The experience made her determined to address the income disparity and gender and social injustice she witnessed.

In 1990, she went to study at the London School of Economics and Political Science. "I loved London. I could escape from the family, lead an independent life and make my own decisions. I never wanted to come back to Hong Kong. My friends there were wonderful. I was president of one of the societies of the Student Union."

She graduated in 1993. At that time Britain was in a recession and, without a British passport, she had no right to stay. "So I came back, with a heavy heart." She went to work at Price Waterhouse Cooper and, after four years, qualified as an accountant. "I found there, as in other firms, a massive racial divide in Hong Kong. There was a white quota for partners; they promoted white people. And there was a Chinese quota, and they promoted Chinese. I was told that I would never be a partner. It was idiotic."

So, she moved to Banque Nationale de Paris, and at this time she met Ravi Gidumal, who would become her husband. He was also a Sindhi born in Hong Kong, who had studied at Island School. Five years older than she, he graduated from Boston University and took over Town House, a company his mother had set up in 1962. It is one of Hong Kong's leading suppliers of homeware, tableware and accessories. The two dated for three years and married in 2000. Her husband's family was more liberal than hers. His mother, aunt and sister all attended university; his sister and an uncle married outside

Shalini Mahtani receives her MBE from Prince Charles, now King Charles III. (© Shalini Mahtani)

the Sindhi community, to an Englishman and an American woman. The family had emigrated from Shanghai to Hong Kong before 1949.

Passports for the Stateless

Ahead of the handover in 1997, Gidumal did a great service to more than 10,000 South Asian residents of Hong Kong. Born in the city, they did not hold passports of India or Pakistan; nor would they be entitled to Chinese passports after 1997 because they were not ethnic Chinese. As a result, they would become stateless.

Together with others from the younger generation of the HK Indian community, Gidumal launched a lobbying campaign in the British House of Commons and House of Lords; The lobby group employed a political campaign firm and was supported by the last British governor, Chris Patten. His charm and persuasion won the day – in February 1997, London agreed to give full UK passports to those South Asians in this predicament.

After her marriage, Mahtani wanted to work in Non-Government Organisations (NGO). "Many turned me away. The only role they saw for me was fund-raising among expatriates, because I did not speak Cantonese. I was not seen for my skills, only for my race and colour."

So, in 2003, she founded her own NGO. It was Community Business, devoted to corporate social responsibility, diversity and inclusion. "Multinational companies loved it. We used standards on these issues in the UK and applied them in Asia."

She published reports on Women on Boards for the Hang Seng Index and the Bombay Stock Exchange. Her NGO conducted research and training on: diversity for women; LGBT+ matters; disabled people; and culture for international companies across Asia.

For her work, she has awarded many accolades. She was made an Asia 21 Fellow by the Asia Society in 2007, received an MBE from Queen Elizabeth II in 2008 and was included as a Young Global Leader by the World Economic Forum in 2009.

Losing Her Beloved Son

On Friday May 29, 2009, she was preparing to fly to India to give a speech at a conference there. Her three-year-old son, Zubin, suddenly fell ill and she rushed him to hospital. He died two days later, of complications resulting from pneumococcal meningitis.

Shalini Mahtani (back row, second left) with her family. Her husband Ravi Gidumal is holding their son Zubin. (© Shalini Mahtani)

"He died of medical negligence. I cannot find the words to describe losing a son. No day passes when I do not understand how it happened. He had no pre-existing condition. No-one asked me for permission to take my son."

The tragedy forced her to stop working. "I do not know what I did in that time, other than just function." She spent time with her daughter, then 18 months old. She informed the board of Community Business of her decision; they continued their work without her. In 2011, she and her husband adopted a third child, a boy.

"Part of me is dead. It died with Zubin."

Zubin Foundation

Following Zubin's passing, friends donated money in his memory. In 2014, a member of the board of Community Business proposed a foundation named after Zubin, using the HK$300,000-400,000 that had been raised. "I told him that I did not care and wanted nothing to do with it. I was not thinking of doing anything again."

But her friends prevailed on her to step forward and play a role. The Zubin Mahtani Gidumal Foundation was established in 2014, with her as CEO. "I wanted to speak for those with no voice. When Zubin was dying, he had no voice, no one helped. I witnessed this. I don't want other people to suffer; although I could not save my child, maybe I can help others. I use the goodwill and networks I had built up with Community Business to help to improve the lives of Hong Kong's marginalised ethnic minorities"

Shalini understands mental health first hand. "I cannot function as before, I feel much pain in my body at times. I work three days a week. When I function, I can function well but not all the time. I need time to replenish." With its office in a former industrial building in Kwai Chung, the Foundation has a staff of 11, including two senior officers who came from Community Business.

The mission of the Zubin Foundation is to improve the lives of Hong Kong's ethnic minorities, reduce their suffering and provide opportunities for them.

Its programmes include: helping women and girls in crisis; providing jobs, internships, opportunities and scholarships; working with parents on parenting, especially for children with special needs; providing mental health counselling service for minorities, in Hindi, Urdu and English; emergency relief, such as food during Covid, and after the March 2021 Yau Ma Tei Fire which killed one and injured 13; and giving out menstruation supplies.

"We found that 13 per cent of (minority) girls missed school because they did not have such supplies. Given free, they relieve girls of

Shalini Mahtani at the entrance of the Zubin Foundation. (© Shalini Mahtani)

a financial burden. In 2020, we impacted the lives of 12,000 people. We were unable to save our own son but could help to reduce the suffering of others."

Influencing Public Policy

Mahtani is an active voice in public policy in Hong Kong. About the administration of the former Chief Executive Carrie Lam, she says that it has done more for ethnic minorities than any of its predecessors. In her manifesto when running for office in 2017, Lam included a whole section on racial harmony. She invited Mahtani to be policy advisor on racial harmony at this time.

"In 2016, we provided a Diversity List of people from the minorities to serve on the Advisory and Statutory Bodies (ASBs). Between 2016 and 2020, we proposed more than 130 people, of whom 25 per cent were accepted; this is significant and shows direct impact.

"I use the goodwill and networks I have built up with Community Business to help to improve the lives of Hong Kong's marginalised ethnic minorities."

From the left, Shalini Mahtani's mother and grandmother: Mahtani with her adopted son: and daughter. (© Shalini Mahtani)

"Our rationale to the government was simple; unless they include ethnic minorities in advisory and statutory bodies of the government, it is not possible to understand their views and therefore address poverty in this community."

As a result of all this and other policy recommendations and engagement, there is much more discussion of ethnic minorities and a budget to improve their situation. "But there is a long way to go. One in four of the ethnic minorities live in poverty. One in three are children. Covid-19 has set the population back, [with] unemployment in [the] food and beverage, airport and construction sectors. It has also intensified the negative stereotypes about them in the community."

Mahtani said that she was deeply grateful for her other two children, her daughter aged 13 and her son aged nine (as of 2021). She derives strength from her Hindu religion. "I believe in life after death. My religion helps me understand that the purpose of life is to improve ourselves and learn from our experiences. But nothing can take away the sadness and loss from Zubin's death."

Hong Kong NGO Donates Goods Around the World

David Begbie

In 2002, a school in Cameroon received a complete library that had been donated by a charity in Hong Kong. When it was handed over, the entire school, from the headmaster down, started "jubilating".

It was one of thousands of donations made each year by Crossroads Foundation, a non-profit set up in 1995 by the Begbie family. Crossroads collects unwanted goods and donates them to those in need.

In the 2019-2020 year, it delivered goods worth HK$117.8 million, half to individuals and groups in Hong Kong and half to 53 countries around the world. A total of 925,339 people benefitted.

David Begbie is a director and one of two sons of the founders, Malcolm and Sally. He has been involved in the work of Crossroads since its inception. Like his parents, he and his family live in the former Perowne Gurkha Barracks in Tuen Mun that is its headquarters. The site covers eight acres, most of its buildings filled with resources which they donate to others.

Making Big Macs in Beijing

Begbie was born in a hospital in Sydney on September 26, 1975. His father was a chartered accountant and his mother worked in public relations. He grew up in a world of humanitarian service. When he was three, the family moved to the Philippines, where they lived for seven years. His parents combined their day jobs with charity for people across Asia and the former Eastern European bloc.

In 1986, the family moved to Hong Kong and soon settled in Silvermine Bay on Lantau Island. The shift to cheaper rent was to facilitate a small import-export business, which would generate the financial support necessary to continue their charitable efforts.

Begbie and his younger brother Josh attended the Hong Kong International School (HKIS), which gave them preferential fees. He studied Mandarin diligently but progress was slow. Exasperated, his teacher said he should go to a place where he would be immersed in the language. In the summer of 1993, he took the plunge.

He spent six weeks making Big Macs on an internship in McDonalds in central Beijing, its first and the biggest in the Mainland. They served 18,000 customers a day, 26,000 on a weekend. "No-one spoke to me in English," Begbie said. "After two weeks, suddenly all the vocabulary I learnt clicked into place. When I returned to Hong Kong, my teacher was blown away."

Meanwhile, his parents' business did not flourish. By 1992, the family bank account had fallen to just US$10. They started looking for other models to support their charity efforts.

Amazingly, in July 1995, that moment came. A disaster in the northeast province of Liaoning changed the lives of the Begbies forever. The worst flooding in 100 years affected two million people and left tens of thousands in need of clothing.

The family was asked to help. They began to collect donations. What started with 19 boxes, soon became 72 and then 136. China's national carrier flew the clothes to Liaoning at no cost. The flood of donations filled Malcolm and Sally's bedroom and then empty classrooms at the Australian International School.

When a more permanent location was required, the Social Welfare Department advised them to form a Non-Governmental Organisation (NGO). It, initially, gave them six rooms in what had been a British Military Hospital (BMH) in Wiley Road, Kowloon. This was how Crossroads Foundation was born. "Within three months, over 10 tonnes came in. We couldn't stop it from starting, and now we couldn't stop it from growing!"

To Join or not to Join?

Begbie's childhood had been one of service. He knew he wished to serve in Asia, but through which channel was yet to be known. For his undergraduate years, he did East Asian studies at Wittenberg University in Springfield, Ohio, including three years there and one year as an exchange student in freezing Harbin in northeast China.

Post graduation, Begbie returned to Crossroads for a two-year placement. His parents were eager for him to work alongside them but wanted the decision to be his own. "They were often on the verge of asking me, but always bit their tongue at the last minute."

It was, however, during that time that Begbie made a trip to Macedonia and Bosnia and Herzegovina to assess the impact of the shipments Crossroads had sent. "I saw the encouragement, hope and practical assistance these shipments offered orphans and war victims. It was everything I had longed to do. When I returned to Hong Kong, I remember standing at the office photocopier, saying suddenly to my parents: 'This is the work I want to be doing for life'. My mother cried."

In order to be of better service to Crossroads, Begbie pursued a Master's degree in Leadership Studies at the Regent University School of Business and Leadership in Virginia.

Business Model

Why has Crossroads thrived in Hong Kong? There are several reasons – it is a city of wealth; it is a global shipping centre and there is no culture of second-hand goods.

"The Excelsior Hotel called us when it closed down. It told us that we could take anything we needed. A bank calls us to say it is moving office and invites us to take all the furniture from 10 floors."

In this way, Crossroads has been invited to collect the entire contents of a hotel wing or a bank building. "Hong Kong is a city with many resources but no large second-hand market or culture."

Another factor is the wealth of individuals and middle-class people who are willing to give away items they no longer want. Hong Kong is a city of migrants, some coming and some leaving.

It is also an ideal point from where to transport goods around the world. "When we ask for space, we often get favourable rates from shipping companies. One company, for example, gives us space for 10

Photo above – In 1983, David in Yugoslavia. Below – The Begbie family in Hong Kong, taken in 1993. (© David Begbie)

containers a year free of charge."

Since they do not have staff overseas, except for a small UK office, Crossroads works with local groups that understand the local language and culture and are accountable for the shipments.

"No one knows where the shoe pinches better than those wearing them. The aid sent is richer, and the deployment more strategic, because of these partnerships.

"The world not only can, but needs to respond at greater levels than it has to date... and it is through these partnerships that transformational joy arrives.

"Imagine the impact when a couple receives a shipment to start a school in their village, or when brand-new, high-end winter clothing reaches those suffering in minus 30-degree conditions, or furniture from a five-star hotel used to established a drug rehabilitation centre. Even the containers themselves can be of use – one is now a medical clinic in a refugee camp."

Half of Crossroads' resources goes to local NGOs and families on social welfare. The balance of their goods has been distributed in over 100 countries.

In its annual report for 2019/2020, it recorded revenue and expenditure of HK$14.416 million. Of donations, HK$4.887 million came from individuals: HK$4.159 million from foundations and charities: HK$2.728 million from the Hong Kong Jockey Club: HK$1.88 million from corporations: HK$544,643 from the Education Sector: and HK$214,070 from the government for Covid assistance. Administration costs accounted for only 3.6 per cent of spending.

Walking a Mile

In 2005, Crossroads celebrated its 10th anniversary. It did not have the funds to follow local custom and host a Gala Dinner in an upmarket hotel. So, Crossroads decided to invite 15 CEOs to the site, strip them of their possessions, wallet and iPhone: give them hammers, nails and bricks and tell them to build a slum. They would sleep on the ground, eat with their hands, and for one day perform the tasks others spend a life doing.

"It was hard to persuade them, so first we picked on our friends," Begbie said. "The 15 CEOs said it was a profound experience. One told me that, in his life, the three most powerful events were his marriage, the birth of his son and this experience."

This experiment snowballed. The CEOs asked Crossroads to organise similar programmes for their staff, as did schools and universities. Soon the topics grew in breadth to include a range of global issues. The United Nations then reached out to see if they could bring their refugee simulation to the World Economic Forum held each January in Davos, Switzerland; 3,000 of the world's most powerful people gather there. "There was no way, the UN told us, that they could bring all these world leaders and show them the reality of conditions in refugee camps. But there was a way to bring the message to them.

"We built a refugee camp with barbed wire and simulated guns and prepared a 90-minute programme. At the start, we feared that no-one would come. I sent an e-mail to invite Sir Richard Branson. He replied the next day, saying he wanted to come. Then many others came.

"Where else in the world can you leverage economic change in a single place and spread the message of 'heart'? Those who came included Ban Ki-moon (then secretary-general of the United Nations), heads of state and, over a 10-year period, thousands of other leaders.

"What makes the experience powerful," Begbie said, "is that the programme is designed, and delivered, not by actors, but by refugees and humanitarian aid workers. One of our cast, for example, is a former child soldier from Uganda who stands up and shares how the militia had surrounded his school to recruit him and other boys. If they did not join, the militia said they would return the next day, kill their teacher and force the students to eat his flesh.

"The goal of these programmes, however, is not shock and awe,

"Our joy is watching empowered people realise
their lives can make a difference."

but rather hope-filled action. Some who have participated have gone on to start NGOs, build schools, volunteer, or provide resources for refugees, or revamped their supply chain to impact the lives of those in need."

There is now a whole suite of programmes on various topics, which have proved extremely popular. Over 200,000 people have attended them since 2005. "Our joy is watching empowered people realise their lives can make a difference."

Global Hand, Global Handicraft

In 2001, Crossroads established a virtual warehouse, in addition to its physical one. This is www.globalhand.org. Anywhere in the world, at any time, people with quality goods and services to donate can offer them on this platform. The recipients are the foundation's network of NGOs in Europe, Africa, Southeast Asia, Central Asia and the Americas.

The foundation also built an online matching system for the United Nations to interact with the corporate sector.

In 2005, it set up Global Handicrafts, as a fair-trade shop. It purchases items from Hong Kong and around the world on a fair-trade basis that sees a fair income go to artisans and producers living in economic need. Buyers can go to the foundation's shop in Tuen Mun, for goods from Asia, Africa, Europe, South America and the Middle East. Or they can shop online.

Volunteer Model

Ever since 1995, Crossroads has retained its volunteer model. All full-time staff are unsalaried. Currently, it has 55 full-time staff from 20 countries, some are gap-year students, others retirees – all choosing to use their skills to serve those in need. Many have worked there for more than 10 years, some more than 20.

At the World Economic Forum in Davos, Switzerland in 2009, then United Nations Secretary General Ban Ki-moon brings other leaders to take part in the "Refugee Experience" organised by Crossroads. (© David Begbie)

In addition, 6,000 people serve each year from the community as day volunteers. "They say that it takes a village to raise a child. This feels like a village. I even met my wife there!"

Begbie said that the inability to hire for competency is sometimes a problem. "People offer themselves and we seek to use their strengths. We would love to have more people. The benefit of our volunteer model is that donated funds go further. For each US$1 we receive in donation, we distribute US$9 worth of goods, if sent internationally, and US$28 if distributed within in Hong Kong.

"People work on an open-ended contract. They can leave if they wish. What binds them is not money but their service of those in need."

At the Crossroads warehouse in the former Tuen Mun military base. (© David Begbie)

Rolling Three-Month Lease

The Crossroads' headquarters is in an old army base in Tuen Mun. Since it moved there in 2004, most of its time has been on a three-month rolling lease. Begbie and his family, his parents and all the full-time staff live on the base. "That was one of the plus sides of an old army base – it came with lots of barrack style housing."

In August 2015, the Town Planning Board sought to reclaim the entire site for housing. After negotiations, Crossroads was allowed to remain on the eastern half of the site. The western half was rezoned for luxury housing.

When the British Army left Hong Kong, it offered many of its sites to the People's Liberation Army. Perowne Barracks was offered to the Hong Kong Police, but it was too big for their needs, and so the land was broken up and given to different institutions.

"Although we have had to give up some of our land for housing, the government has been very supportive and promised to reprovision us, if necessary. We could not have done this work without their generous provision of this land."

In 2007, he received the Hong Kong Humanity Award (co-organised by the Red Cross), for his devotion to being a "voice for the voiceless".

7 Pakistani IT Wizard
Has Global Ambition

Ali Shamaz

A young engineering student at the Hong Kong University of Science and Technology (HKUST) has a global ambition: "I want to make the biggest homework digital platform in the world."

Ali Shamaz is the co-founder and designer of Fan{task}tic, a product he plans to offer to the schools of Hong Kong in the autumn of 2021. He aims to raise US$1 million in venture capital and offer it to schools first here, then in Taiwan area, Britain, the United States and other places.

"My Mother Tongue Is Cantonese"

Ali was born on June 8, 1999, eldest of four brothers of a Pakistani couple that settled in Hong Kong in 1997. "Previously, my father worked in a jeans factory in South Korea for three years. Then he and my mother came here and decided that they could make something. His brother was also living in Hong Kong – he has eight children."

His father earns HK$14,000 a month cleaning cars. "His Cantonese is poor, so that he cannot get a better job." The family also receives social welfare benefits. They lived in rented apartments in walk-up buildings until 2015, when they moved into a public housing unit in Tsz Wan Shan.

His father and mother speak to each other in Urdu, the national language of Pakistan. "But my mother tongue is Cantonese, which I started learning at kindergarten," said Ali. "There were five minority students out of the 30 pupils there. The rest were Hong Kong Chinese. I can speak Urdu but cannot understand everything my parents say."

There was a similar proportion of minorities at his government primary school. "My classmates made jokes about our appearance but it was not serious. I enjoyed my time there, especially art, music, football and badminton. I did not like the traditional classes." He played guitar, drums and piano.

He was, and is, a devout Muslim. "Up to six years ago, I went to the mosque five days a week from 4pm to 6pm. I read the Koran in Arabic and memorised about five per cent of it. I do not eat pork, smoke or drink alcohol. I pray twice a day. I fast during Ramadan. But I could not this year [2021], because I was working too much. I needed the energy you get from food."

"Become a Doctor"

Ali attended a Cantonese-language government secondary school in Prince Edward and was one of the top students. His favourite subjects were maths, physics and physical education. "The maths lessons were in English, so I could improve my language ability."

His mother wanted him to become a doctor. "She was typical of ethnic minority parents. They want their children to be lawyers, engineers or doctors. These jobs have money and status and make their parents proud. But I hated the sight of blood. I wanted to be an architect."

The Pakistani community is close-knit. The family attended events at the Pakistan Club in Princess Margaret Road, in Kowloon. They visited the homes of other members of the community.

"Initially, my parents wanted to introduce me to a cousin from Pakistan as a possible wife. This was common practice 20 years ago. The Immigration Department would grant a visa to such a person who married a member of the community here. But now society is more open. My parents do not talk about this now."

Must his future wife be a Muslim? "That is usually the case. But you cannot force someone to convert. It must be her own choice."

Wins First Prize

His aim was to study architecture at Chinese University of Hong Kong (CUHK). In the Diploma of Secondary Education, he got a 27, a high mark, with 5** in maths, physics and chemistry. "But I received only three in Chinese. I slipped up there."

"But, at CUHK, I failed in the interview. I did not have enough knowledge of architecture." He was accepted into the engineering faculty of HKUST.

"I do not study much. I find classes so boring and traditional." In 2017, he took part in a Start-Up competition; few others did. He was not diligent in his course work and failed in three courses. But he did enough to pass the exams and stay in the university.

In 2018, he took part in the Alibaba Hong Kong B2B E-Commerce Youth Festival and won the first prize.

In 2019, he applied for and was given a year off school. It was a tumultuous year. His mother died of a heart attack. He and three friends from CUHK set up Phoennovation. Its first project was Suit Up! It used Artificial Intelligence (AI) to help men find the clothes they wanted. "You put in your body weight, size and other data and the programme found clothes for you."

He received a grant of HK$100,000 in venture capital from the STEP (Science and Technology Entrepreneur Programme) scheme for IT companies.

Fan{task}tic

The team has since stopped work on Suit Up! and turned its energy to Fan{task}tic, the programme for schools. He is one of four co-founders. He has a 75 per cent share and is the designer. The Chief Technology Officer holds the other 25 per cent. Three students from CUHK work as developers. They have hired nine interns from HKUST, which covers their costs.

"We aim to create the biggest homework digital platform in the world. The programme will create unique homework for each student and enable the teacher to receive feedback on each of them. It will save his time in preparing and grading homework.

"The preparation of homework can be done by machine. It is meaningless for the teacher to do it. Our programme will enable

ALI SHAMAZ

Founder of
Fan{task}tic &
Phoennovation

"We aim to create the biggest homework digital platform in the world. Fan{task}tic will create unique homework for each student and enable the teacher to receive feedback on each of them. It will save his time in preparing and grading homework." (© Fan{task}tic) teachers to save time and energy for what they should be doing."

They are pricing the product at HK$240 per student per year, starting with schools in Hong Kong and aiming down the line for ones in Taiwan area, the US and UK (for GSE and O and A levels).

To achieve these ambitious plans, he needs US$1 million. "Such funding is normal in the US but hard in Hong Kong. I have talked to venture capital companies and Angel Funds.

Rating Hong Kong

How does he rate Hong Kong as a place for start-ups? "In pace and efficiency, Hong Kong is very good. People work quickly.

"But the government is putting start-up funds into projects, not people. It is too conservative. It should put the money into people who are passionate about what they are doing, as Taiwan area does. I plan to apply there next year.

"A start-up means risk, uncertainty and working all-night. You must believe in yourself and what you are doing."

Initially, his parents opposed his IT work. But, when he won the Alibaba competition and earned money, they started to support him.

During his life, he has visited Pakistan three times to see relatives. "I could not live there. It was so quiet, with nothing to do. You just stay at home. After his retirement, my father will stay here and not go to Pakistan.

"I would like to experience other countries, but Hong Kong will remain my home."

His brothers are not as academic as he is. "My advice to them is to do what they like and reach out to others. No-one knows what the world will be like after 10 years. Many jobs will be replaced."

Pakistani friends of his have been stopped by police on suspicion of dealing in drugs or other crimes. "I carry a laptop, so the police do not stop me."

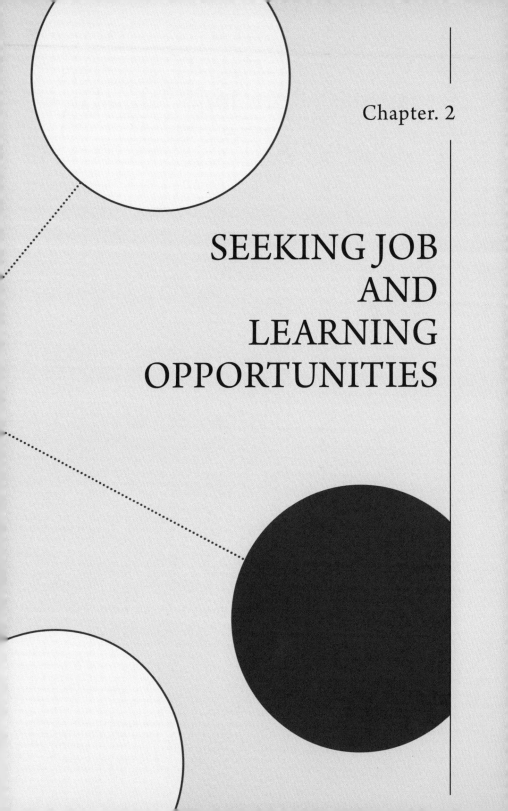

Chapter. 2

SEEKING JOB AND LEARNING OPPORTUNITIES

8 Japanese Runs Judo School in Hong Kong for 55 Years

Takeo Iwami

In 1966, Takeo Iwami moved to Hong Kong in 1966 to open the first judo dojo run by a Japanese. Today, 55 years later, he is still running it, on the 12th floor of the building that houses the Sogo department store.

It has 100 students, half of them French and the others Japanese, Hong Kong Chinese and other Caucasians. "Judo's value lies in the regimen it teaches anyone, of any age. It is about discipline, respect and dignity," Iwami said. Into his 80s, he remains an active teacher.

In 2008, the Emperor of Japan awarded him "The Order of the Rising Sun, Gold and Silver Rays" for his services in promoting the relationship between Hong Kong and Japan through judo.

But Iwami could as easily have been a member of Parliament and minister in the Japanese government. A graduate of the elite Waseda University, he served for eight years as private secretary to Yasuhiro Nakasone, who became the country's Prime Minister from 1982 to 1987.

The turning point came in summer 1962. Iwami was one of hundreds of students on "A Ship for World Youth" visiting ports in Asia. They arrived in Hong Kong and stayed at the YMCA in Salisbury Road. Iwami visited the city's judo hall; the teacher was an imposing English police inspector. He challenged him to a bout; to the amazement of the onlookers, the diminutive Japanese threw the policeman to the ground.

This decided him to bring his beloved judo to Hong Kong, an objective he achieved four years later.

Always Cold and Hungry

He was born on February 26, 1937 in Sendai, the largest city in the north of Honshu, the main island of Japan. His father was an engineer in the national railway company; the family, with five children, lived in a company house. Since the government considered his father's job essential for the war effort, he did not have to enlist in the army.

Sendai was an important industrial city and the target of American bombing raids. So Iwami's father moved his family to a rural area near Ichinoseki in nearby Iwate prefecture. There they were safe from the bombing.

"Life was very poor. I was always hungry. On August 15, 1945, I heard the broadcast of Emperor Hirohito announcing the end of the war. It was a very hot day. I understood what he meant. In the countryside, we did not need to go to bomb shelters. My family survived the war. But many died, even those in the shelters. We lost friends and relatives."

Rural areas recovered more quickly than the cities after the war. Iwami was able to attend primary school, equipped with text books, a piano, an organ and other musical instruments. "I had a good education, despite being cold and hungry and short of clothes. My favourite subjects were literature and sociology; I hated mathematics."

He first took up judo at high school; his teacher was a policeman. He showed a photograph of him and four other students, in their dark school uniforms, who practised judo together. They do not have the faces of a defeated nation.

In 1955, he graduated from high school and spent two years as a 'ronin' the Japanese term for graduates who have been unable to enter a university. On the third attempt, he passed the entrance exam for Waseda, to study commerce. To improve his English, he read *The Old Man and the Sea* by Ernest Hemingway.

To finance his studies, he found a job at Taisei Construction, one

The young Takeo Iwami working to earn money and support his family. (© Takeo Iwami)

of Japan's biggest building firms, as a night security guard. The site was part of a new subway line for Tokyo city. "My professors were very nice. They allowed me to snooze in class."

At Waseda, he was an eager sportsman, especially athletics and wrestling. He became the All Japan Wrestling Champion and a member of the national wrestling team; it toured the United States. He was not a model academic student.

One night on duty at the construction site changed his life. On patrol at midnight, he met Americans who had been drinking at bars in the nearby Shinjuku district. He fell into conversation with the visitors. One was Edwin Hewitt, an executive of Pan Am, one of the world's largest airlines at that time. Hewitt found out that he was a Waseda student and invited him to his house.

It was there that he met Yasuhiro Nakasone, who was Hewitt's guarantor in Japan. The two men became friends. Iwami became his private secretary, a part-time post he held for eight years.

Judo Missionary

It was in 1966 that he decided to come to Hong Kong, to spread the practice of judo. He persuaded Taisei Construction to hire him as a civil engineer, on local terms.

"Nakasone-san gave me his blessing. I said that Hong Kong was nearby and a very important city, as a trade and financial base of Asia. It would be good for the future of commerce with Japan and improve the relations between our people. Nakasone-san gave me two business suits. We have kept a close relationship with his family, visiting them when we go back to Japan."

In 2008, it was his son Hirofumi, then Foreign Minister, who presented the order on behalf of the emperor.

Iwami opened his first Judo dojo in Prince Edward, with a monthly rent of HK$60. The sport was new to Hong Kong, with the first course introduced in 1940 aimed at foreigners. In 1960, Fung

Ngai, with some expats, organised Judo courses at the YMCA. In 1964, Koon Fook Cheung established the Far East Judo Club and Stephen Tsai Teh Bei set up the Judo Department in South China Athletic Association. Iwami was the first Japanese to establish a Judo dojo in Hong Kong. The Judo Association of Hong Kong, China was set up in 1970.

For Iwami, it was always a labour of love. While students paid fees for classes, these were never enough to cover the rental charges, electricity, water and other costs. He saw it as his mission to spread his beloved practice to a foreign country, especially one so close to Japan. He always had to subsidise the dojo from his own earnings.

His first female student was a striking Hong Kong lady named Amy. She came from a wealthy family that was preparing to emigrate to the United States. They decided that they had to learn self-protection in their new country.

Her father was a civil engineer, in the same field as Iwami. He invited him to his house, where Iwami met the five children. He and Amy fell in love; they married in 1976.

Her family moved to California and prospered. The other children became doctors and dentists. But Amy stayed in Hong Kong. One reason was that, born in the chaos of World War Two, she did not have a birth certificate and other documents required by the US Immigration Department.

A more romantic explanation is that she preferred her sweetheart to the sunshine and rolling beaches of California. She herself has become a blackbelt and helps to manage the dojo. They had one son, Ryuma.

Learning Japanese

From 1981 to 1986, Iwami returned to Japan. He was offered a well-paid job in a construction company. Another reason for returning was to enable Ryuma to attend a school there and become fluent in the language. He also speaks Cantonese and English; he studied at Chapman University, in Orange, California, in the United States.

During their absence, Hong Kong colleagues continued to run the dojo. After the family's return in 1985, they bought a property in Tai Hang Road for less than HK$3 million. It is now worth 10 times that amount.

Iwami was helped to find the property by Ronald James Blake, one of his judo students. A civil engineer, Blake settled in Hong Kong in 1965 and took part in many landmark projects, including the Cross-Harbour Tunnel and the Mass Transit Railway. He served as Secretary for Works in the Hong Kong government from 1991 to 1995. Blake introduced Iwami to the property agent who found the apartment.

In 1986, they moved the dojo to Causeway Bay, home of many Japanese companies and residents. In 1984, Iwami set up the Toyo Security & Building Management Company Limited, of which he is the chairman and Ryuma is manager.

Its office is on the 12th floor of the East Point Centre in Causeway Bay, which also houses the Sogo department store. It won the contract for the security and management of the whole building. Iwami is one of the few people in Hong Kong with a licence to carry a gun; he stores it in a safe in his office. The dojo is on the opposite side of the corridor on the same floor.

Father, mother and son were all skilled in judo and taught at the dojo. Amy is a black belt. For 45 years it has been a family business.

Iwami never thought of retiring to Japan. "My family, friends and dojo are all here. The staff of my company are very loyal. We work closely together."

Character, Etiquette and Manners

The dojo is a large room of 160 square metres. On the wall is a photograph of Dr Kano Jigoro, who founded judo in 1882, when he was 22. In 1900, he established rules and regulations for referees of

In 2008, Takeo Iwami received from the Japanese emperor "The Order of the Rising Sun, Gold and Silver Rays" for his services in promoting the relationship between Hong Kong and Japan through judo. (© Takeo Iwami)

competitions.

"Through training in techniques of judo, a practitioner can nurture his physical and mental strength and gradually embody the essence of the Way of Judo – good character, right etiquette and manners, self-control and the betterment of the nation and society," said Dr Kano.

Next to the photograph is a wooden shrine to a Japanese deity. Since non-Japanese may not wish to bow to it, Iwami diplomatically placed on the wall flags of the countries from where his students come. So, they can bow together before and after the class.

Since 1966, the dojo has attracted on average between 100 and 150 students, including adults and children. The classes run two hours for adults and 90 minutes for children. The peak number of students was 200.

Now there are 70-80 adults and the same number of children.

"My family, friends and dojo are all here.
The staff of my company are very loyal.
We work closely together."

Takeo Iwami with his students. (© Takeo Iwami)

The main language of instruction is English, because of the variety of nationalities. They also use Japanese phrases. About half of the students come from France, the country in the world where judo is most popular. The others are Hong Kong Chinese, Japanese and other Caucasians. The dojo accepts people of all levels of skill. They have classes almost every day.

"Judo's value lies in the regimen it teaches, for any age," said Iwami. "It is about discipline, respect and dignity. There is less hitting than in other martial arts. You do not get bruises that much as it is more self-defence when you throw and lock people. You have to learn to fall. It helps you learn how to fall without getting hurt or banging your head."

For him, it was a matter of great sadness that the sport is in deep decline in Japan, the land of its birth. "The young people want to play soccer. There is less and less judo in schools. Soccer is a quite different sport. Few people want to become judo teachers outside Japan. People do not understand the spirit of it correctly."

But that does not diminish the contribution he made to thousands of students, from all over the world, who learnt from him in Hong Kong since 1966.

9 Teacher of Japanese Savours Retirement in Hong Kong

Katsuo Uemura

In July 1994, Katsuo Uemura arrived in Hong Kong with his new Hong Kong wife and started to teach Japanese at the Extramural Department of the Chinese University of Hong Kong (CUHK). Nearly 30 years later, he is enjoying his retirement in his adopted home.

He works two mornings a week at The Japan Society of Hong Kong, organising courses and exhibitions to encourage Hong Kong students go to university in his home country. But he has no plans to move there.

Rice and Apples

Uemura was born on March 2, 1953 to the family of a farmer in Hachinohe, Aomori. It is the most northerly prefecture of Honshu, the main island of Japan. Temperatures fall below freezing in the winter.

"We had a small farm on which we grew rice and apples for sale and vegetables for our own consumption," he said. The apples of Aomori are famous all over Japan; the prefecture accounts for 56 per cent of the nation's production.

Uemura had three sisters and two brothers. All the family had to help with collecting the rice and apples at harvest time in the autumn. The harsh winter prevents a second crop; so, farmers take work in factories during the winter months.

Theirs was a poor family. Uemura was one of five students in his class of 40 at primary and secondary school to receive free stationery from the local government.

"Growing up, I had no clear ambition. I liked reading books but was little use on the farm. My parents were not so strict with me. I grew up with a sense of freedom. My family allowed me to choose my future."

After junior secondary education, he attended a technical college, 30 minutes' walk from his home, under a newly organised five-year education system. "I did not like it because I did not want to do a technical job. Mainly I read books in the library."

Delivering Newspapers

He wanted to go to Tokyo to further his studies but had to find a way to pay for it. He found a job with *Asahi Shimbun*, one of Japan's biggest newspapers, as a delivery boy. The country's major papers have a dense network of bringing their product to readers before they go to work in the morning. This meant that, like his colleagues, Uemura had to get up at 04:00 and deliver the papers before 06:30 in the neighbourhood allocated to him. He did it again between 14:00 and 15:00 for the evening edition. "Young Japanese do not want to do this work now because it is so exhausting. So, foreigners do it, such as Vietnamese."

Asahi Shimbun provided the fees that enabled him to study history for four years at Sophia a Jesuit-run university, in Tokyo. He attended classes and did his homework before and after delivering the newspapers.

He wanted to change his studies before graduation. To earn money, he worked for six months in a Honda car factory. "Other manufacturers only accepted high school students as part-time workers. Honda alone took on university graduates and drop-outs for this kind of work."

His next college was International Christian University, where he studied Social Science for four years. He had decided by then that he wished to become a teacher of Japanese to foreigners.

He went to Waseda University in Tokyo for graduate studies in Japanese, including grammar, the classical language and how to be a teacher. He taught a class of 20 foreigners, 10 of them from Hong Kong. One was a young lady who stayed in Japan to work; she returned to the campus to take part in student activities.

The two fell in love and married in 1992. They decided that they would live in Japan and not Hong Kong. "My mother-in-law did not like Japanese [people] and said that we had done many bad things [in wartime]."

The health of his mother-in-law deteriorated; Madame Uemura had to spend two months in Hong Kong to look after her, followed by two in Tokyo with her husband. The two decided that this was not tenable and they should move to Hong Kong.

He applied to CUHK and the University of Science and Technology as a Japanese teacher; he made two separate visits by plane for the job interviews. After he secured the post at CUHK, they moved in July 1994. "For me, it was not a sacrifice. I was not so happy at the school where I worked at the time."

Adapting to Hong Kong

"I had no idea about Hong Kong, I had no image. All I knew was what I had seen in maps. I knew no Cantonese and my English was limited. For shopping, my wife bought things for us."

In the two months before the autumn semester at CUHK, he took buses and ferries all over the city to learn about his new home. "I felt very comfortable. The air was good." Fortunately, when his mother-in-law met him, she formed a positive opinion of her new son-in-law.

For the next 19 years, he worked at CUHK, teaching both full-time and part-time students. There were on average 2,000 part-time and 100 full-time students annually.

There are two main reasons for Hong Kong people to study Japanese. One is to enable them to study at universities in Japan and, in some cases, stay on to work. They may also wish to work in the many Japanese companies in Hong Kong.

The other reason is that many people love everything Japanese – including films, music, magazines, cartoons and food. In 2018, 2.21 million Hong Kongers visited Japan, an astonishing three in 10 of the population. It is the country's fourth largest source of tourists. This fascination stimulates people to study the language.

Japanese has three alphabets, one of them Chinese characters imported from Chang'an (near to the site of modern-day Xi'an) during

Photo above – With his students on an outing. Below – With his colleagues at Chinese University. (© Katsuo Uemura)

the Tang Dynasty (618-907 AD). So, like other Chinese and South Koreans, Hong Kong people have a head start in learning the language, far ahead of other foreigners. They know the meaning, if not the pronunciation, of many words.

"From kindergarten, Hong Kong students learn foreign languages and can adapt easily," Uemura said. "But they find some sounds difficult, like the difference between 'n' and 'l'. Students from north of Fujian do better, but those from the south cannot master it. But, if you study hard, you can overcome the obstacles."

In 2013, he reached the retirement age of 60 and retired from CUHK. Since 2015, he has been working three half-days a week at the head office of The Japan Society in Central, on different projects. In August 2018, he became a full-time member of staff, before returning to part-time in 2020. His current title is the principal of its Japanese Study School.

Emigrating to Japan?

One of his projects is to encourage Hong Kong people to study at universities in Japan. He has arranged an intensive six-month programme to enable them to reach the language level required to enter university. "In the entrance exam, they can choose to take some subjects in English, like maths, science and general knowledge. So. they should not worry about not being able to pass."

In 2020, 500-600 Hong Kong people were studying in Japanese universities, at undergraduate and graduate level.

Japan has one of the lowest birth rates in the world. So, since 2009, its government has been encouraging foreign students to stay on and work after graduation. Uemura has this advice on finding a job. "From the third year, students should start looking for work. Foreigners do not understand this. They continue to study hard and wait for graduation until they start looking. It is too late then. Most important is to find a company willing to train you. Hong Kong and Japanese

With his colleagues at the Japan Society. (© Katsuo Uemura)

firms are not the same. Not so important is academic achievements but a student's strong points and character and his understanding of the company. Much of what he studied is no use at work. In this third year, look at different companies and do not study too much. In the summer holiday after the third year, many students have an internship. If it goes well, they can start work immediately after graduation.

"Hong Kong students must also take part in university activities and have more to write on their resumes. Companies want to see if they have leadership qualities and can work in a team. Japanese students party for two years. In the third year, they become very serious and look for work. A foreign student can also do part-time work, to understand Japanese society and connections. To enter Japanese society is not easy but you can do it if you put your heart in it."

"We Japanese find Hong Kong an easy place
to live. We do not experience anti-Japanese
prejudice. When I walk along the street,
I am simply an Asian."

The work culture at Japanese companies demands that colleagues often leave and drink together, before going home. Some foreigners find this hard to adjust to.

But, despite the falling birthrate and an ageing society, Japan does not welcome immigrants. "Japanese society is closed. Few people go abroad to study. It is very hard to emigrate there or obtain the right of permanent residence."

Retirement

Uemura greatly enjoys his retirement. "I spend three hours a day watching NHK (the Japanese state television company) and reading Japanese newspapers, especially the *Asahi Shimbun*. Then I spend three hours walking outside, including hiking. I feel very comfortable.

"We Japanese find Hong Kong an easy place to live. We do not experience anti-Japanese prejudice. When I walk along the street, I am simply an Asian.

"Before, we had a plan to retire in Fujian province but not now. We will stay in Hong Kong. We own no property in Japan."

The couple have no children. When he was working full-time, his wife got up to prepare breakfast for him, as well as a lunch box with Japanese vegetables. Now he works part-time, he does not get up early. He has breakfast with his wife; they watch the morning drama on NHK. Together they speak Japanese. His knowledge of Cantonese is limited.

10

Australian Veterinarian Treats Hong Kong Pets for Decades

Lloyd Kenda

Since he arrived in Hong Kong from Perth (via Singapore and Sydney) in 1995, Lloyd Kenda has treated thousands of dogs and cats and brought happiness to their owners.

"You can never take for granted the special bond a person has with their pet," said Kenda. "Most have a very unique bond with them. You know that they care, especially if one is unwell. In Hong Kong and worldwide, more and more young couples are opting to have pets together before, or even instead, of children! Their pet is well and truly family, and it could be said that a pet gives you a lot less grief than children!!"

In 1998, he took over what was the very first small animal veterinary clinic in Hong Kong. Now he is looking after the pets of the children of those who were his clients over 20 years ago. "It is very nice to be a part of that circle".

He lives with his wife Tanya and daughter Lucia in Wan Chai. Lucia is studying at primary school in Hong Kong. Their son Alessio is studying medicine in London. In the future, he will be treating humans, not animals.

Baby Kangaroos in the Laundry Room

Lloyd was born on January 27, 1967, one of two children of a high school biology teacher in Busselton, then a town of 20,000 people in the southwest of Western Australia. It is close to Margaret River, an area famous for its wines; it produces a fifth of the country's premium wines.

Baby Lloyd was delivered by Doctor Kevin John Cullen, who founded Cullen Wines with his wife in 1971. It would become one of the state's most famous vineyards. When Lloyd was one year old, the family moved to the city of Perth, the state capital. In 1973, the family opted for the "good life" moving 30 kilometres east of the city to a small town called Glen Forrest. They lived in a semi-rural, hobby farm area with three acres of land.

It was here the young man spent his formative years and developed a lifetime love of animals. "We had many animals – chickens, ducks, sheep, horses, dogs, cats and birds. Our house became a shelter for rescued animals, such as joeys [baby kangaroos], possums who had lost their mothers in traffic accidents or been attacked by dogs. I was very fond of kangaroos, horses and horse-riding, and always had our family dog 'Skippa' by my side".

"My parents loved all animals. I grew up with joeys in the laundry room, animals all over the property. They made no money from them; it was not a commercial farm. In actual fact, all this must have cost my parents a fortune." His father worked full time – with the benefit, as a teacher, of long holidays.

Lloyd went to the local primary and secondary schools. He did not enjoy school but saw it as a means to an end; he was a talented student and came top of his class, with straight As. For his matriculation exams, he studied maths and higher maths, physics, chemistry, economics and English.

In 1982, his sister moved to the United States. In 1984, his parents divorced, so he was largely left to himself as he finished high school and started university.

After graduation from school, he was uncertain what career to pursue. He enrolled in the science faculty of the University of Western Australia; for three years, he studied human biology and psychology.

While he was there, he decided to become a veterinarian. So, he enrolled in the veterinary school at Murdoch University in Perth. It was one of only four veterinary schools in Australia at the time. There were just 44 students in his year's cohort; everyone knew everyone. The years at university were fun, despite the hard work!

"We studied all kinds of animals – large and small, pets and farm, wildlife and exotic. I preferred working with pets – primarily cats and dogs – and wanted to become a surgeon. Murdoch University was new and progressive, with excellent teaching staff and facilities. One of the highlights was doing surgery. In those days, we did do real surgery on live animals. It was excellent training for us – but, of course, this type of practical teaching is not permitted now."

In those days, the greatest demand was for veterinarians who treated large animals, like cattle, horses and sheep. "Not all students wanted to do it. It was heavy, physically demanding work, with long hours and poor pay, living in isolated Australian communities – usually away from friends, family and support." Unfortunately, worldwide, the suicide rate among vets is the highest amongst all professions. Living and working in isolated areas significantly contributes to this.

"It is due to the demands of the clients, the physical pressure, long working time and low salaries – and the fact that vets have easy access to euthanasia drugs. It is an unfortunate combination of factors. One of my classmates from Murdoch University has had great success in developing a programme to reduce these suicides in young vets. It is, however, something that we need to do within our profession to support each other. Luckily, more and more is being done to help vets support each other... but there is still a long way to go."

Finding a Job

He graduated in 1992 but there were few jobs for vets in Australia in those days. Many of his classmates left to work in London, where there was greater demand and better salaries.

, That year he married his sweetheart, a student of law, and he moved to Sydney, Australia's largest city. He started a job there shortly after graduation – but it lasted all of three days. The clinic director was a mature vet with strong opinions; it became apparent very early that the two would not be able to work well together!

It was an era without internet or mobile phones so person-to-person contact was the best way to proceed. He compiled a list of veterinary clinics in the Sydney area and spent a month visiting them one by one, travelling by bus. "It was the height of summer and very hot. I went door to door, with cold calls."

He found a job in the inner city that took him on, first as a two-week locum and then full-time. He greatly liked the job and the working experience.

Go to Asia

"My wife finished her law degree. The lure was to go to London, to gain experience, where there were better job options and to also have an adventure. Both of us were qualified to work in the UK. We felt that it was now or never!

"However, when living in Newtown, Sydney, we used to buy fruit and vegetables in Chinatown and always walked past a branch of HSBC. Hong Kong sounded like an interesting place, the handover was looming and neither of us had ever been there. We decided to spend a year in Asia before going to London."

Thanks to an introduction from a vet in Perth, he was able to secure a job at Mount Pleasant Animal Hospital in Singapore. The director there, Dr Tan, was the first local Singaporean vet; he had received his training in Scotland and owned a very busy progressive practice. "I loved it. It was so different. As a young man, I had not travelled very much at all and actually took my first plane internationally when I was already 18. The clinic was busy. I worked hard and learnt much. I particularly relished the experience of living in and amongst another culture."

Trying to stay with the plan of a year in Asia before heading to London, after five months they applied for jobs in Hong Kong, where the qualifications of both were recognised. They moved to Hong Kong in early 1995.

Hong Kong – First-Time Pet Owners

At that time, Hong Kong had about 20 veterinary clinics. The first small animal clinic, now called the Valley Veterinary Centre (VVC), had been set up by a Scottish jockey and vet named Doctor Allan Auchnie in the 1970s. With no veterinary college in Hong Kong, nearly all the practitioners were foreigners, with a few Hong Kong locals who had studied overseas and returned to work back home.

Lloyd was employed by a veterinary group with clinic branches in Tuen Mun, Yuen Long and Sheung Shui and started work on April 1, 1995. His wife found work in a law practice. So, Hong Kong was a good choice for both of them. "We both loved it here."

"In those days, very few of the clients in the New Territories spoke English, so we communicated through a nurse interpreter. Many of the owners had never had pets before, so they had much to learn. Basic animal husbandry was lacking – feeding, exercise, all needed to be explained. Many put their pets in a cage and back in a cupboard like a toy after they had played with them! The clients were very willing to learn and do their best for their new pets.

"Making work even more interesting, I saw diseases I was not used to seeing. Diseases like distemper and heartworm I saw regularly – many diseases that were no longer seen in places like Australia due to good vaccination and preventative medicine programmes were common in Hong Kong.

"On the positive side, the owners really embraced the idea of having a pet. If you explained well, they were fascinated and eager to do the right thing for their pet, which was now considered part of the family".

At the end of 1995, he moved to Hong Kong Island to work in Wan Chai and then in 1997 to work with Anderson & Hawken (who had bought Dr Auchnie's clinics when Dr Auchnie retired), with clinics in Mongkok and Happy Valley and kennels in Pokfulam. The two owners were Australians approaching retirement. In 1998, Kenda proposed leasing the Happy Valley business from them. A month later, they asked if he wanted to buy it!

They explained that they had received an irresistible offer for their land in Pokfulam, to build an approach road for the planned Cyberport development. They wanted to take the money and "retire" in Australia.

"They told me that they feared the Hong Kong dollar/US peg would be broken and asked for payment in US dollars. Not having any great savings accumulated by this stage, they agreed to be paid over a period of time, unstated. We shook hands and that was it. There was no contract. It was a gentleman's agreement."

So, in October 1998, he became the third owner of the clinic in Happy Valley and renamed it as Valley Veterinary Centre. He bought the practice, equipment and the stock inside but not the building, which was rented. It had a loyal base of clients, some of whom knew Dr Auchnie and his wife June.

In order to pay the debt as soon as possible, in fear that the US dollar peg would go, Lloyd worked non-stop until the debt was cleared. In 2000, their first child, Alessio, was born. A year or so later his wife stopped full-time work as a lawyer. She then taught part-time at Hong Kong University.

Open 365 Days a Year

In the years since then, the Valley Veterinary Centre has been the centre of Kenda's life. Wanting to keep the practice small, he has hired only one other vet, as well as full-time and part-time nurses and receptionists. He does all the administration and business management work himself.

"I want to keep the practice personal and friendly. I know all the animals and owners myself. I like the relationship with clients. The clientele is typical of the demographic of Hong Kong island – a mixture of all different nationalities, locals and expats. Nearly all our clients are happy to converse in English with me, so I can talk directly to them. I meet new people all the time. They come from all over the world. I greatly enjoy this. I really would not like to be tucked up inside an office seeing the same few faces every day!"

The clinic is open 365 days a year and offers 24-hour emergency

Lloyd Kenda at the Valley Veterinary Centre. (© Lloyd Kenda)

communication with a veterinarian, including Christmas and New Year, Chinese New Year and Easter! It offers medical, dentistry, diagnostic, radiography, vaccinations and surgical care. When the time comes, they can also perform end-of-life procedures to humanely put the animal to sleep and arrange their cremation.

In 1998, after completing exams in small surgery, Lloyd was admitted as a member of the Australian and New Zealand College of Veterinary Scientists. "In addition to professional qualifications and memberships, I have accumulated a deep understanding of Hong Kong from an animal's perspective, including the myriad diseases and afflictions encountered here."

Initially the workload was very heavy. He and his colleagues were on 24-hour call. "In an emergency, sometimes in the middle of the night, we would see patients, perform surgery such as caesarians, and then be back at work at 8am ready for the day. We did everything."

Today the workload is still demanding, but, because of the opening of several 24-hour specialised clinics staffed with doctors and nurses around the clock, now in emergency cases, Lloyd can refer sick animals to these clinics for specialised treatment; these include CT scans, MRIs, treatment of spinal injuries and high-risk cases.

"In the early years, I worked every weekend and missed out on a lot of sports days and family events with my son. Now, in a normal week, I am off on Tuesdays and Sundays. I can attend more weekend events with my daughter. The days at work are busy and often challenging, but never dull! On average, I do two surgical procedures a day and consult four hours in the morning and five in the afternoon. I enjoy it, working in a friendly environment with good staff and wonderful clients and, of course, being surrounded by animals. These days we have far better drugs and equipment than in the past. They make the lives of animals so much better."

He also treats rabbits, birds, turtles and other exotic animals; he was trained to look after them. But now there are specialised clinics for exotic pets in Hong Kong so this work is less and less.

Dealing with Clients

During his 26 years in Hong Kong, Kenda has witnessed a boom in the market for domestic pets. They have become an integral part of society, treasured by everyone from children to adults to the elderly.

"Hong Kong is an affluent society. The middle class can afford to keep pets and spend on them. Most of my clients are very good owners and want to do the right thing."

But not all clients are easy to deal with. "There are only a few, but some are unreasonable and can be very nasty. They feel very entitled and get very frustrated if they do not get the outcome they want. An old dog will die, this is inevitable. The hardest part is to deal with grieving people. Ninety-nine per cent of problems is communication. You must explain that a pet does not live forever and will eventually die no matter how much money you have or how advanced the medical treatments are – that is life"

He said that there had been an exponential rise in complaints against veterinarians, in part because the internet has enabled people to learn a little information and get poor advice from social media. This has emboldened them. "It is great that pet owners want the best for their pets and are willing to educate themselves, but sometimes a little information without the full background knowledge can be detrimental to their understanding. There is so much outright incorrect information, particularly on social media, that often we have to re-educate the client!"

In one memorable situation, a dog died whilst its owner was out of Hong Kong. The dog was presented to the clinic by a family member but the dog was already dead. After the owner returned to Hong Kong late that night, she went to the practice and tried to smash the door down. "When I got there, I was relieved to see police at the scene. It was quite a threatening situation. In other cases, clients have been very verbally abusive to my team and myself, they have broken and smashed things and made awful threats. This is not the side of being a veterinarian that people think about or even want to know about!"

This pressure is the reason many veterinarians leave private practice after only six to seven years and go to work in government, academia, big pharma – anywhere away from the direct public pet interface, where they can still use their knowledge. "This is because of the grief they receive from their clients. They deal with heavily charged cases and receive many verbal threats and emotional blackmail. Compassion fatigue is real!"

Fortunately, dangerous clients are few and far between. On a day-to-day basis, his greatest physical danger comes from crazy cats. "They are worse than dogs. They have sharp claws AND teeth!"

"We both love Hong Kong and the many friends we have made here. It is clean, organised, has excellent transport, it is efficient, and people-friendly."

Kenda likes the Hong Kong environment and being able to look into the far distance.
(© Lloyd Kenda)

No Retirement

Lloyd and his wife have a younger daughter, Lucia, born in 2010. "There is no retirement in the foreseeable future! I will work as long as I can and as long as I still enjoy it."

Before COVID-19, the family used to visit their relatives and friends in Perth about twice a year. It is a seven-hour flight, with no time difference.

"We have strong bonds there and we want our children to know their family and appreciate Australia. I never go away for more than 10 days at a time otherwise it is just too hectic on return back to Hong Kong. This is the downside of working for yourself and running your own business."

He misses the sports of his home, especially cricket and Australian rules football, and Australian music and the ability to see small live music acts regularly. "Of course, we also miss the lack of space. Where I grew up, I could spend an entire day without seeing anyone. Our family had a reasonably big house but with a very big yard at the back. That was normal."

But he and his wife have no plans to live in Perth. "We both love Hong Kong and the many friends we have made here. It is clean, organised, has excellent transport, is efficient, and people-friendly. You can be in the central business area, then on hiking trails in 15 minutes where you find wildlife and serenity in the jungle. There is nowhere in the world like that. We love that aspect."

He also likes its geographical location, enabling the family to visit his son in London and his relatives in Perth easily.

He and his wife belong to the Hong Kong Cricket Club in Wong Nai Chung Gap Road, where they enjoy the cricket and the peace and quiet. "It is our backyard."

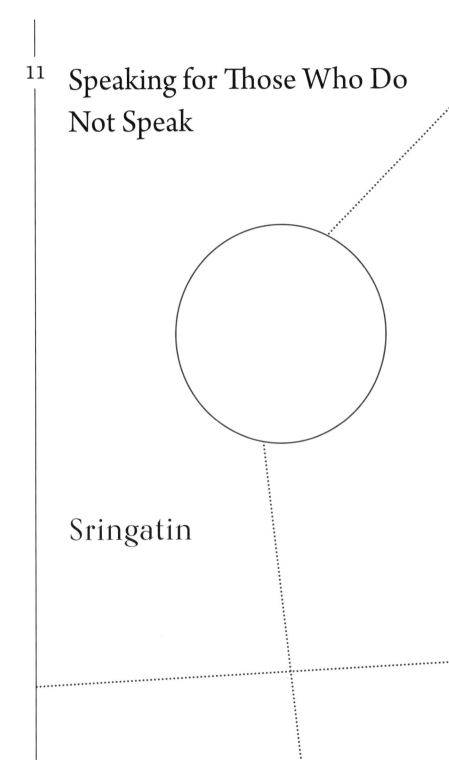

11

Speaking for Those Who Do Not Speak

Sringatin

Sringatin is a spokeswoman for the 183,000 Indonesian maids of Hong Kong. They are, after the 200,000 Filipinos, the second largest minority in the city. She is chairperson of the Indonesian Migrant Workers Union (IMWU). Since 2002, she has lived 19 years (and counting) of her life in Hong Kong – not by choice but because she lacks the money and connections to find a good job at home.

"We pay a very heavy price for working here," said Sringatin. "If people had a good salary or their own land in Indonesia, no-one would come here to work as a maid."

Hard Childhood

She was born on August 2, 1980 in Blitar, a village in East Java, that was the home place of Sukarno, the first president of the independent Indonesia.

Her childhood was sad and eventful. She was one of six children; her father was a farmer and her mother ran a small business. After the family went bankrupt, her parents moved to a remote area of Sumatra under a government transmigration programme; they took her and her brother. But the land they were given was poor and full of mosquitoes; when she was six, both her parents died of malaria.

The area had neither medicines nor health care. An elder sister collected her for a journey of six days by bicycle and bus back to their home village, where she went to elementary school. A teacher adopted her into her family and helped to pay her school fees through primary and secondary school – education in Indonesia is not free.

"The family treated me as one of their own children." An intelligent student, she completed 12 years of education, followed by a six-month course in finance and taxation; she had computer skills and a knowledge of accounting.

With these assets, she expected to find a good job. But she was disappointed. "I tried everywhere – banks, motor showrooms and big corporations in palm oil, mining and timber in Sumatra. But I had no connections and was not willing or able to pay the 'red packets' you need to get to the front of the queue."

The best she could do was work as a cleaner in a hotel in Sumatra. "I could have done the job of the supervisor – but she was a relative of the hotel manager. My adopted mother advised me to join the army or the police, but I was not interested."

She had an elder sister who had gone to work as a domestic maid in Hong Kong in 1998 and advised her to join her in the city. She was in the middle of a 10-year stint with her second employer; she cared for an elderly person in the family and was well treated.

"The places promoted by the government were Hong Kong, Brunei, Malaysia and the Middle East. Of these, the people of Hong Kong had the best reputation, in terms of treatment of their maids."

Move to Hong Kong

The next step for her, as for other applicants, was a three-month training course with a recruiting agency in Indonesia. This cost the first seven months of her salary that was paid by her employer. She was offered Taiwan, Singapore and Hong Kong and chose the last because of her sister.

"The course was like the army. We got up each morning at 05:00 for physical exercise. It was not useful. We were taught a little Cantonese by a maid who had worked in Hong Kong. We were taught cleaning and a little cooking, how to make fresh vegetables and steamed fish in the Chinese style. We could not choose our employer."

Her first one, in 2002, turned out to be a nightmare. The couple was extremely wealthy; they had three grown-up children, several apartments and five cars. She lived in their Sham Shui Po apartment. She was paid HK$2,000 a month, instead of the legal minimum of HK$3,670 and given one day off a month, instead of the statutory Sundays and public holidays.

They had another maid, a Filipina, who received the legal wage.

"I had to clean all five cars every day. My world was the apartment, the food market and the car park. Why did I have to clean cars on Sunday, while my friends could enjoy themselves? Everything was strange, I knew no-one. On the plus side, I had my own room where I could read Indonesian newspapers and I was not physically abused.

"My job was to clean and cook. My boss was polite and gave lai see at Chinese New Year. We communicated in Cantonese. I cannot explain why such a wealthy woman was so mean."

In addition, her boss forced her to eat pork, which is forbidden to Muslims. "She did not eat beef and ate pork. I had to eat the same as the family. It was very difficult to accept."

She complained to her elder sister and said she wanted to leave; but her sister said that this would involve many more fees. So she completed her two-year contract. With the second employer, she was not so patient. She terminated after two months. "On rest days, I had to work before 08:00 and after 21:00."

Then it was third time lucky. Now knowing the law, Sringatin agreed everything in advance with her employers, an elderly couple with a son, a daughter and a dog. "They were very nice. I had my own room and bought a computer and a guitar. On Sunday, I went to work with the Indonesian Migrant Workers Union (IMWU). I enjoyed the free time and music. The elderly couple helped me with my Cantonese; they told me many stories. The downside was that the contract did not specify the working hours; these turned out to be from 07:00 to 22:00 or 22:30. Every day was the same, the same duties."

In 2009, she returned to Indonesia. With the money she had saved, she built a modest house for herself in her home village. She hoped to start a business or a coffee shop or buy a farm. But she did not have enough money; and her native village was too poor to support new businesses.

So, in 2010, she returned to Hong Kong; since then, she has had two employers. She has become increasingly involved with the IMWU. She has helped to represent other Indonesians who have been

Sringatin helps a fellow Indonesian who suffered from unfair treatment. (© Sringatin Atin)

physically or sexually abused, not properly paid or suffered other forms of injustice.

The most famous case was that of Erwiana Sulistyaningsih. During 2013, she was physically abused for eight months by her employer Law Wan-tung, a mother in her 40s. She was given no day off, worked 21 hours a day and slept on the floor. Her wounds became infected; Law did not allow her to see a doctor.

On February 27, 2015, a District Court found Law guilty of 18 out of 20 counts of abuse of Erwiana and two other maids. The court sentenced her to six years in prison and the payment of HK$800,000. She was given parole in November 2018. "Despite the verdict, Erwiana has not received one cent of compensation. Law does not want to pay. Her lawyer is appealing, I think."

Erwiana lives in Indonesia and is receiving counselling. "She still

"We care for and love the old people. They miss the warmth and closeness of their own children. We want to make everyone happy. But no-one cares for our feelings. How about our parents and our families?"

suffers from the ordeal. Her sight is not clear and she suffers from back pain."

Helping Her Sisters

Sringatin became chairperson of the IMWU. "We would like to see the law and contracts specify the working hours of a maid. If not, then they should specify that we have the right to eight hours of sleep and three hours of private time per day. Erwiana slept two hours a night, others sleep four-six.

"And, if you are looking after a disabled person or one who needs 24-hour case, you may have no proper sleep. Everyone is your boss, including the pet."

She also challenges the regulation that maids must live in the homes of their employers. "Some maids sleep on the floor, in cupboards, in the bathroom, the kitchen and the storage room. One slept in a room with 11 dogs and developed skin infection. They have no privacy."

She said that, with the consent of the employer, maids should be allowed to stay elsewhere; this would give breathing space to both parties. In addition, domestic maids should, like other foreigners, be allowed to apply for permanent resident status after seven years; current law does not allow them to apply.

She estimates that 10 per cent of employers treat their maids badly.

"We understand that Hong Kong women work long hours to get a better life. Everything costs money. We care for and love the old people. They miss the warmth and closeness of their own children. We want to make everyone happy. But no-one cares for our feelings. How about our parents and our families?"

She said that most victims of ill-treatment did not want to speak out; it was not easy to take complaints to court and how long would it cost in time and money?

Asked about the toll their work abroad takes on the personal life of the maids, Sringatin said: "Indonesian maids stay between four and 20 years in Hong Kong. The average is 10 years. The youngest is 20 and the oldest is 60. They send between HK$1,500 and HK$4,000 a month to their families at home and keep HK$500 for themselves, for personal spending, such as a smart phone to call their family.

"The pandemic and lockdown in Indonesia increased the need of the families for money. About 60 per cent of the maids are married, some as young as 17. They see their families once a year. If they have children, they leave them with their husband and grandparents. Some need to hire helpers at home to take care of their parents. In these circumstances, a gap develops between mother and children; contact via iPhone is not enough."

She estimates that one per cent of the maids marry in Hong Kong, to a Chinese, Indian or Westerner.

"The culture is very different. The working hours and living arrangements make it difficult to develop a relationship. In Indonesia, if a non-Muslim marries a Muslim, he or she must convert to Islam."

Two decades in Hong Kong have taken a heavy toll on Sringatin's own hopes of marriage and a family. "You need time and familiarity to develop a relationship. I have had long-distance relationships before. They did not work. For marriage, I will have to be in Indonesia. You need to have commitment.

"My dream is to go home and buy land, which I can live off. But I cannot buy land in my native village, where my house is, because it is too expensive. Indonesia has no social welfare, housing or medical benefits."

12

Indonesian Has Helped Her Sisters in Hong Kong for 15 Years

Kristina Zebua

What happens to a domestic maid in Hong Kong who becomes pregnant and is dismissed by her employer?

They turn to PathFinders, an NGO set up in 2007 to assist them. Kristina Zebua, an Indonesian, has been helping the migrant community for more than 15 years. She is the Community Education Manager of PathFinders.

"In 2020, we dealt with 400 cases and 1,100 mothers and babies. We give them three options – legal termination, adoption or having the baby. Many of the mothers do not have the information they need. I am working to educate and empower them," she said.

In 2003, Kristina obtained a Masters of Divinity from Jakarta Theological Seminary. The next year Mission 21, an evangelical order based in Switzerland, invited her to work at Christian Action in Hong Kong, to help migrant workers. She has been here ever since.

From Remote Island to Social Action

Kristina was born in 1979 in Nias, an island off the west coast of Sumatra. Unlike the rest of Indonesia, more than 80 per cent of its 750,000 people are Protestant Christians, a result of conversion by German missionaries.

Hers was a comfortable middle-class family. Her father was an engineer in the regional construction company and her mother a teacher, principal of a kindergarten and later an official in the Social Welfare department.

Kristina had four brothers and sisters. Two were adopted from a couple who were members of the family but could not afford to raise them.

"Our house was part of a family complex. For dinner, we had 10 people. The house was always open. My parents were leaders of our 'clan'. People came to ask them for advice and money," she said.

At home, the family spoke Bahasa Indonesia, the national language, rather than the local Nias dialect. Her parents wanted the children to be well prepared for life outside the island. "I can understand the Nias language but cannot speak it."

Kristina attended kindergarten and primary school at Catholic institutions in Nias. When she was 13, she asked her parents if she could attend a model boarding school opening in North Sumatra. It was funded by associates of then President Suharto; it was one of the most luxurious schools in Southeast Asia. From Nias, it was an eight-hour journey by ferry. "I told my parents that Nias was too slow and too calm for me. I am not calm; I like a fast pace."

Her parents were reluctant to let her live so far from home but recognised her determination. So, they said that, if she acquired the A grades needed for the top stream, they would allow her to go.

She studied hard and achieved the grades needed; she was one of 28 students to qualify for her class, a third of them women. The school had a total of 228 students. It had a well-equipped campus, with an excellent library, a cinema and sports fields. For Indonesia, the class sizes were small.

Since the founders were from the army, the school was highly disciplined, with a military uniform and a tight schedule, including physical exercise.

Her favourite subjects were English, Bahasa Indonesia, maths, physics and chemistry. She had her first experience of prejudice – people from Nias were considered low-class and poorly educated. They asked why, as someone from Nias, she was studying in the school.

"The experience of discrimination made me stronger. I was outspoken and the students chose me to represent them."

After completing three years of study, she had to choose between two public universities in Bandung, west Java and the theological seminary in Jakarta, the oldest one of its kind in Indonesia, set up in 1934. Her preference was for one of the two universities; her school friends were going there.

But her parents wanted her to attend the seminary; they and a cousin would cover the tuition and living fees. She took the entrance exam and passed. So, she found herself in the capital city, 1,300 kilometres from home and where she knew no-one.

Theology and Counselling

She spent five years at the seminary, studying theological science and educational and pastoral counseling. She threw herself into social and political life, joining demonstrations against the rule of President Suharto.

During the summers, she did pastoral internships, at the Centre for Seafarers and on international ships, where she improved her English. She also provided pastoral care to women who had divorced and to students at school.

"On graduation, I did not want to become a minister but a teacher or to study for a Ph.D. I became a research assistant to a professor and a resident mentor for the female students in their first year. I was considering further study in Holland or Australia."

Then, out of the blue, came the offer to work in Hong Kong – to help migrant workers in difficulties who had taken refuge in a shelter and needed counseling. "I had never thought of Hong Kong. It was not on our radar at all. I did not speak Cantonese."

The offer came from Mission 21, the mission society of the Reformed Protestant Church in Switzerland. It works as an international, charitable institution in Africa, Asia and Latin America, in cooperation with over 70 partner churches and organisations and over 100 projects across the globe.

She was excited by the project but fearful of working in a city she knew nothing about and so far from home. "I called my mother. She said: 'What do you want?' She was an educator, very open-minded."

In July 2004, Kristina came to Hong Kong for a preparatory visit. Her job would be to work at the To Kwa Wan Service Centre and Shelter. It helps foreign domestic workers exploited by unscrupulous employers and agents. It provided basic food, shelter and counselling and taught labour rights, computer training and language classes.

Alone

In August 2004, she moved to Hong Kong and stayed in the tiny studio that had been used by her predecessor in the job. Finding it too small, she moved into an apartment in Choi Hung of a Home Ownership Scheme project. The rent was HK$3,500 a month. She would stay there eight years.

"The first three years were very hard. I felt alone. I knew no-one other than the people from Mission 21. They were Europeans and Chinese, very nice, but they were not from my culture. I missed my family and I missed Indonesia. So, I threw myself into the work. I liked it so much.

"I tried to learn Cantonese, but Hong Kong people were not friendly. When I spoke the language, they laughed at me and my mistakes. So, I have not learnt it."

Her employer was Christian Action (CA), founded in Hong Kong in 1985. Initially, it managed the Kai Tak Vietnamese Refugee Camp and provided training and job placement services at all 10 refugee camps in the city. Since then, it has expanded to provide services to migrant workers, refugees, and the poor and needy, including free meals.

Demand for the classes Kristina organised was so great that CA moved them to its headquarters at Choi Hung. Every Sunday, over 300 domestic helpers attended the classes. Kristina was the driving force in establishing the programme.

She wanted the workers to return home with knowledge to start a business and find meaningful employment opportunities. They could then afford to raise their own children, take hope into their communities and pass on the values and skills they learnt in Hong Kong.

In 2006, at Kowloon Union Church, she married her sweetheart, a freelance photographer from Indonesia, who had been her best friend there. He comes from south Kalimantan in Borneo. Since then, he has lived in Hong Kong on a dependent's visa thanks to his wife.

His parents are Muslim and have not acknowledged the marriage. "He is close to my parents. If we had a Muslim marriage, I would have to convert to Islam. We considered that, but decided against it, just for the sake of pleasing his parents. We should live our own lives."

Needs Unlimited

The mission Kristina took on was without limit. Domestic workers took refuge in the shelter in To Kwa Wan because of abuse by their employers and the employment agencies which had hired them. They needed both physical and psychological support. "When you see the need, you cannot stop at what your contract requires you to do."

Some domestic workers took legal action against their employer, a process that can last up to a year. This meant that they stayed in the shelter for 6-12 months, while the case was being settled. "Their money may not be enough. They needed to get something out of this." So, she provided classes offering different skills.

"I was so involved in the work that, on Sundays, I went to Victoria Park to talk to other ladies on their day off. We opened another centre for classes for those who were not in the shelter. My husband was one of the first volunteers to help me."

She continued this work with Christian Action for eight years, until 2012.

Helping the Unborn Child

In July 2012, she moved to PathFinders. This was established in 2007, when co-founders Kylie Uebergang and Melissa Mowbray-d'Arbela rescued four babies born to migrant women. They identified a gap in Hong Kong society where women and babies go undocumented and unprotected. They believed that no child should be born alone and

Helping the domestic maids who become pregnant. (© PathFinders)

deprived of medical support, shelter and identity.

As of 2021, it had served almost 7,000 babies, children and women. A charity, it provides child protection, counselling, shelter, food, health, education and legal support. Its website says: "Many migrant domestic workers are women of child-bearing age who lack reproductive health knowledge. PathFinders adopts an educational and preventative approach towards ensuring every pregnancy is considered and planned, enabling a clear, stable and brighter future path is established for every child. Without systemic and policy change, we know the problems PathFinders tackles will likely escalate with the number of MDWs [migrant domestic workers] employed in Hong Kong."

It receives its funds from private and corporate donors, mostly expatriate. It has 20 staff, including expatriates, Chinese and

"I must do outreach with them and provide education. They have power within themselves." (© Kristina Zubua)

Indonesians. In 2019, its revenue was HK$9,868,357, mainly from project income, general donations and fund-raising events, according to its annual report.

Kristina is now in her second stint with PathFinders. During the first, from July 2012 to December 2016, she was a senior case manager. This meant that she was on the front line, helping the women who had become pregnant.

She said that, while several NGOs helped domestic workers who had been abused or not paid, PathFinders was the only one dedicated to those who had become pregnant.

"The fathers are Chinese, European, American, Asian and African. Often their boss ends their employment or they leave of their own accord because they believe they cannot work properly. Under the law, they have the same rights as Hong Kong women. The employer has no obligation to look after the baby.

"As case manager, I explained their rights to them – adoption, legal termination or continuing. Only a minority choose the first two, for religious and cultural reasons. Most want to keep the child."

Of those babies born in Hong Kong, only five per cent obtain HK citizenship. For this, the father must be a Chinese and he must make a formal declaration of his paternity in a court.

Those who have a valid visa can remain here for the birth. "For those who overstay, we help them to surrender to the Immigration Department, which issues a document recognising this. They are waiting for deportation." The Hong Kong government does not consider Indonesia or the Philippines as countries eligible for applications for asylum.

Mother and baby face significant obstacles after their return home. "There is a stigma against mixed-race children. Some families accept them if there is a husband, but in most cases there is not. The family see them as bringing trouble and making life harder. Some families refuse to accept them. We help them settle back in Indonesia."

Kristina sees her mission as educating and empowering the

women. "Many do not have the necessary information (regarding birth control). So, I must do outreach with them and provide education. They have power within themselves." She has recruited 104 Indonesian and Filipina migrant workers as "ambassadors" to help with her outreach work. They devote Sunday, their single day off, to educating others.

In 2020, PathFinders dealt with 400 cases, involving 1,100 women and babies. Of them, 62 per cent were Indonesian, 30 per cent Filipina and the rest were South Asians.

For 18 months until the end of June 2019, Kristina took an 18-month holiday. It was a time to spend precious time with her family in Indonesia and to rest from the pressure of the work.

Then she returned to PathFinders as community education manager. "I very much like the work. I regret not speaking Cantonese," she said.

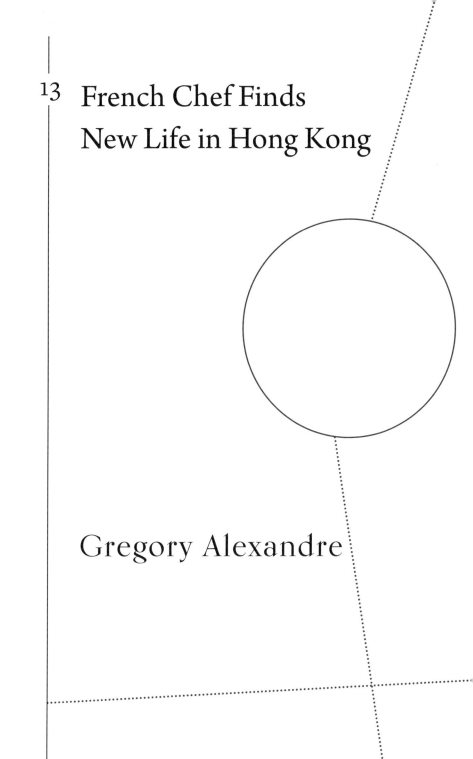

13

French Chef Finds
New Life in Hong Kong

Gregory Alexandre

In November 2010, Frenchman Gregory Alexandre opened Fleur de Sel, a restaurant, in the heart of Causeway Bay with no bank finance or outside investment. He gave it three months to survive.

Eleven years later, in 2021, he owned two restaurants in Hong Kong and a company importing French craft and organic drinks.

Fleur de Sel started to make a profit after 12 months. "I have been able to do here what I could not do at home," he said. "In Hong Kong, you can set up a company in four hours. In France, it takes four months. There are too many rules and regulations."

"I feel more at home here than in France. The time passes very quickly. It is a dynamic city. I feel welcome and secure and there is a good quality of life. I learnt a great deal. People are very open-minded. In France, people mistakenly think they are the best at everything."

Fleur de Sel has only a small number of tables and a staff of six. "I want to keep it small and personal. When clients come, they know they will receive personal attention. They like that. It is not too big. Most restaurants in Hong Kong do not provide such attention."

Growing up over a Restaurant

Alexandre wants to create in his restaurant the ambience in which he grew up, living above the 40-square-metre brasserie (bar/ restaurant) which his parents ran in Suresnes, a western suburb of Paris where he was born in April 1979.

"It was open from 07:00 to 23:00 every day of the year, except for a month's holiday in the summer. We lived on the second floor. I liked the ambience. It was like a village.

"My parents knew everyone. In the morning, our customers were workers and at lunchtime those in office jobs. They told us their stories and their problems, family and finance. My father was a very good listener. Some clients had no money and paid at the end of the month, when they received their wages. I met people whom I had never met outside. The downside was that my brother and I saw little of our parents."

Alexandre was an average student and graduated from secondary school at 15 years old. "I did not know what to do. So, my brother and I followed my parents into the restaurant business. I attended a Hotel School at Saint-Cloud and did internships at different hotels across France.

One was a large hotel in Deauville, a popular seaside resort in Normandy and one setting for Marcel Proust's novel *A La Recherche du Temps Perdu (In Search of Time Lost)*.

"I was one of four students there. We were delighted to work in this famous hotel, close to the sea. In a kitchen, there are four grades of staff, with the chief cook at the top and us four at the bottom. Unfortunately, I had to work with a man who had held the same job there for 30 years and never been promoted. He put so much pressure on me that I left after two weeks."

The next assignment was more successful, at the Grand-Hôtel du Cap-Ferrat, A Four Seasons Hotel, close to Nice, on the French Riviera. This is one of the wealthiest and most popular resorts in Europe. The Rolling Stones and many other celebrities own properties there.

"It opened my eyes. The hotel had many foreign clients, including from Italy, Japan and Argentina. I had to start speaking English. I learnt the meaning of top cuisine. Our restaurant had one star on the Michelin ranking. We served excellent local produce and fish that had been caught the night before. The taste was first class." He stayed there for six months.

He learnt the system of gastronomy in the country which, with China, ranks at the top of the world's cuisine. "France had about 12 master chefs. All the young trainees wanted to work with them. If you applied, you had to wait three-to-four months to have the opportunity."

"What Am I Doing Here?"

In the winter of 2002, Alexandre began to think about working abroad. He applied to restaurants in the United States, South Africa and the Antilles; he sent his curriculum vitae but received no reply.

Then his professor at Saint-Cloud told him that the French consul in Hong Kong, Serge Mostura, was looking for a cook at his residence. Since Mostura was in France at that time, the two men met. "He was sympathetic and diplomatic. I liked him. I was just 22 years old. So, I signed a contract, at HK$17,000 a month. I had no idea about Hong Kong or Asia. Because of SARS, I delayed my arrival from January to early May 2003."

When he arrived, he had a big shock. The house was at the top of The Peak, with a panoramic view north and south of Hong Kong island. "I was the only chef in the kitchen. Two Filipino maids worked in the house. I knew no-one in Hong Kong and was far from my family and friends. My English was poor and it rained all the time. I asked myself: 'what am I doing here?'".

The first four months were difficult, especially to work without the colleagues he had always had in France. He had no easy way to contact his family at home. But gradually, he settled in.

Twice a week, the consul's chauffeur drove him and Madame Mostura to the markets of Wan Chai. "I found almost everything I needed, both items I was familiar and new products I discovered for the first time. It was a voyage of discovery."

He lived in the consulate and was on call all the time. The consul used to invite up to 16 people for dinner, a dozen for lunch and up to 60 for cocktail parties where he awarded medals.

"If he invited the Chief Justice, I had to prepare something special. Fortunately, everyone liked French food. I also had to learn to make bread and pastries, as the consul wanted to say his was prepared on the premises."

Alexandre's grandfather was a baker who used to get up at 04:00 each morning to make baguettes and pastries. "I never knew him but I was happy to learn.

"Sometimes the consul invited guests on the weekends. I had no fixed holidays, except when the consul was away for six weeks during the summer. I was on a local, not an expat, contract. I took short holidays to Vietnam, Thailand and the Mainland, never more than a few days."

Alexandre had the chance to meet French master chefs when they visited Hong Kong, working briefly with them at the Mandarin and Shangri-La hotels. He stayed two years with the consul before moving to Macao.

Robuchon a Galera

In January 2005, he went to work as a sub-chef in the restaurant Robuchon a Galera, opened in the Lisboa Hotel two years earlier by Joël Robuchon, one of the greatest chefs of the 20th century, who operated more than a dozen restaurants in cities around the world, including three in Tokyo. In 2016, they held 32 Michelin Guide stars, a record for any restauranteur. Robuchon died in August 2018, aged 73.

"Robuchon trained all the big chefs. All the young ones wanted to work with him. It was a very good experience to work in Robuchon a Galera. The Lisboa was one of the biggest hotels in Asia, I had 1,300 colleagues."

Robuchon went to Macau four times a year with a team of five. They spent a week preparing 12-15 dishes for a Gala dinner for 30-35 guests on a Saturday. The cost ranged from HK$3,000-$6,000. Alexandre lived in an 80-square-metre apartment close to the hotel, costing HK$3,000 a month. The work was gruelling, with one day off a week, when he came to Hong Kong. As in Cap-Ferrat, he could work with world-class chefs to make meals for the wealthiest clients.

Monaco's Largest Yacht

In February 2006, Alexandre decided to take a holiday. He returned to France and had spent a week with his family; then, the telephone rang. He was invited to work on the yacht of a millionaire in Monaco, on the Riviera. They wanted him to start the next day – so much for the holiday!

His new place of work and residence was the Lady Moura, the largest yacht berthed in Monaco, 105 metres long and owned by Saudi-Arabian businessman Nasser Al-Rashid. It had two helicopters, four side boats, a staff of 70 and seven cooks; four worked only for Al-Rashid and his private guests.

Here Alexandre had an inside look into the life of the super-rich. "Of the cooks, three made food for the staff, two Filipinos made Arab food for the owner and we two French cooks made Western food. Actually, Al-Rashid only ate Arab food, so we shared the Western food among ourselves."

The yacht was parked in Monaco most of the time, with a side trip to nearby Cannes for the annual Film Festival. "I was shocked by the wealth. The owner had 12 bodyguards, a doctor and a chauffeur. But you get used to it and it becomes the 'normal'. It is like the bubble in which the rich in Hong Kong live, with maids, a chauffeur and visits to luxury shops. This is not real life." He worked on the yacht for two months.

In May 2006, he returned to Hong Kong to his former job as cook to the French consul. This time he had an additional task, as manager of the house and responsible for major renovations to the ageing building.

He had an improved salary of HK$22,000 a month and an

A French gateau with many layers. (© iStockphoto)

apartment in Aberdeen to give him privacy from the consulate. He worked there for four years and four months, until August 2010.

Taking the Plunge

That summer he returned to France to see his parents, recently retired. He decided the time had come to take the plunge and open his own restaurant, specialising in crepes. During this holiday, he spent a week with a chef friend in Brittany learning to make crepes.

He returned to Hong Kong with two large boxes of crepes. He was living in an apartment in Fu Ming Street, in the heart of Causeway Bay. On his way home one evening, he noticed part of the second floor was empty. He contacted the landlord and signed a contract to lease the space, at HK$45,000 a month. It is a prime location, close to Times Square and the Causeway Bay MTR station.

It was a big gamble. He had no bank financing nor outside capital. He invested some of his own savings and received some funds from his family. The renovations cost HK$300,000.

"I said to myself that, if the business went badly, I would close after two-to-three months. The early months were very difficult. Friends came once or twice and then not again. Gradually, our reputation spread through word of mouth. We did no marketing in the traditional or social media. It was very stressful. After one year, the restaurant became profitable." He works six days a week, with Monday the day off.

In July 2015, he set up a new company, French Concept, to import and distribute craft and organic drinks from France, including cider, beer, liquor, spirits and alcohol-free wine, in Hong Kong and Macao. Then he opened three more restaurants; he later closed two of them. The third, Bouillon Bistro Parisien, in Pound Lane, Sheung Wan remains open (at time of writing).

Helping him in Fleur de Sel is his wife, whom he married in 2013. She was working in the cosmetics section of SOGO Hong Kong; the two met at a friend's birthday party. They have no children.

His clients are 40 per cent expatriates and 60 per cent local people. "The local people especially like to come back and see people they know."

More at Home

He is grateful to Hong Kong for giving him opportunities he could not have had at home. "People are open-minded and more accessible. I have learnt so much here.

"When I go home, I see how different the mentality is. My family and friends tell me about their lives and I listen. I do not tell them about my life here.

"Life in Hong Kong is very fast. It never stops. I enjoy this pressure, which forces you to do new things. Since I arrived, more and more young Europeans have come to Hong Kong, not with an expat package but to try something on their own. It is like the American dream used to be. You can choose your own destiny."

"Hong Kong is a dynamic city. I feel welcome and secure and there is a good quality of life. I learnt a great deal. People are very open-minded." (© LinkedIn)

14

Indian Director Makes First Bollywood Film in Hong Kong

Sri Kishore

Sri Kishore grew up sleeping on the floor of a modest police apartment in southern India. He spent 10 years as an electrical engineer working in factories around the region.

In 2021, he launched the first Indian Bollywood film in Hong Kong, *My Indian Boyfriend*, which he directed with an Indian and Hong Kong crew. He guided them with a mixture of Cantonese and English, Hindi and Telugu.

The film took five years to make. It was delayed by the difficulties of an Indian trying to persuade people in Hong Kong to invest in his project, then the city protests and the COVID-19 pandemic.

The Cantonese-language film was a commercial success, with wide coverage in Hong Kong and 80 performances in cinemas over five weeks. It was being dubbed in Indian languages for release in India, Malaysia and Singapore.

It was his fourth feature film. Next, blessed with a Hong Kong wife, in 2021 he was writing number five, *Buddha in Hong Kong*.

Childhood

Kishore was born on August 15, India's Independence Day, in 1980, in Nalgonda in the south Indian state of Telangana. It is 90 kilometres from the state capital, Hyderabad.

He is the eldest of three children of a family of the Vishwabrahmin caste; their ancestors were goldsmiths. His father was a policeman and his mother a housewife. "Our family was poor," said Kishore. "Unlike other civil servants, my father never took bribes. Others bought houses early in their career but my father had to wait until he stopped working; he used his retirement money to buy his house."

The family lived in a cramped government apartment. "The whole family lived in a medium size room. We children slept anywhere." They attended a local private English-medium school, with modest fees. It had no sporting or cultural activities and no toilet – only academic lessons. He was top of his class.

"The teachers gave the lessons in English but the students asked questions in Telugu, the local language, and the teachers replied in Telugu." He loved dancing and painting; but these he could only do at home, practising in front of a black-and-white television and painting, with a pencil only – no colours – with his mother on the doorstep.

In 1992, his father sent him to a large private school, also English-medium. It offered a wide range of facilities, so that he could dance and paint. He won prizes for these two skills. "In this school, you had to speak English, even in the playground. It was hard for me in the first two years."

Electrical Engineering

After he graduated in 1995, his father proposed he study electrical engineering; since he had no clear of his future, he agreed. It was the start of 10 years in this field.

First, he obtained a diploma in the subject at a college in Bellary in Karnataka state, which borders Telangana. He learnt Kannada, the local language. "I really enjoyed my three years in college. It was a new life, meeting new friends in a different city."

On graduation, his father sent him to work at an electrical transformer factory owned by his brother near Nalgonda. All the staff were members of the extended family. Kishore sent all his salary to his father.

"The factory was in a forest. All of us lived on the site. My uncle did not let us watch television or films. He wanted to cut us off from the world. It was like a prison. He was a bad manager and would not even allow us to wear shoes, which he considered showing off."

During his four years there, he pleaded with his parents to allow him to leave. But his father insisted that he stay there. His mother whispered: "run away".

He followed her advice. One day, with 200 rupees (HK$20) in his pocket, he ran away to Mangalore, a large port city in Karnataka.

He worked there for 18 months in an electrical engineering firm. Next was a company in the same field in Bangalore; the boss promised him a salary of 6,000 rupees (HK$600) a month – but, when he arrived to take up the position, he was paid just half that.

"Over the next eight months, I did not have enough to eat. I became very thin. When I went home, my mother saw this and cried. 'Stay here and do what you want,' she said."

He stayed two months, regained the lost weight and taught dancing in summer classes. Then his father forced him to go back to his uncle's factory, to make money.

Escape into Films

He stayed there for six months, alone and miserable, before running away a second time. His destination this time was Hyderabad, capital of Telangana and the second biggest film-making centre in India; its nickname is Tollywood, after Bollywood in Mumbai, which ranks first. In 2018, India produced over 1,800 films, more than three times the 577 in Hollywood.

He found a well-paying job in a factory making electrical transformers but devoted more and more time to film. After a few months, he left the job. A man who lived in the same building worked in multi-media; he taught Kishore how to edit film.

The two became friends and invited actors and cameramen to make five- and 10-minute films which they submitted to the Hyderabad Film Festival. All were selected and screened and received media coverage.

"I earned nothing from these films. I was living on savings. I did not smoke, drink or party. I did not take trains or buses but walked everywhere, even in 38 degrees. My friends all had Nokia mobile 1100 phones, the latest fashion. I did not. I was having fun. I had no plan or strategy."

Dancing in Hong Kong

In 2007, a friend moved to Hong Kong to teach Indian dance at California Fitness in Lan Kwai Fong. He invited him to come too, saying that it was a good, regular salary.

Still bent on making a feature film, Kishore declined. He finished a script of a horror film and spent eight months to arrange a meeting with the actress he wanted to star in it. "She rejected it, I was very disappointed." So he accepted the offer of his friend in Hong Kong.

On May 28, 2008, he took an aeroplane for the first time in his life, from Hyderabad to Mumbai and from there to Hong Kong. His friend met him at the airport. "I had seen nothing like it. Everything was so tall. I did not know where the streets ended and the shopping malls began."

For the first six months, he concentrated on the dance lessons, 16 hours a week for a salary of HK$12,000 a month. He stayed in his friend's apartment.

"I had a good time. I spent time getting to understand the city. Bollywood was hot in Hong Kong at that time, so I was a celebrity to some."

In his spare time, he stayed in touch with the film industry in Hyderabad and learnt about digital cameras. From 2008 to 2011, he saved HK$350,000, which he used to buy a small house in Nalgonda, his home town.

He returned to India to make his first feature film, a mystery thriller *Sasesham*, which lasted two and a half hours, with a group of passionate friends. Since he had no money, he found friends who funded the production cost of HK$400,000. "It was a commercial success, earning HK$1.2 million. But the distributor cheated us. The friends received back their seed money, but made no profit."

Sri Kishore loves making films. (© Sri Kishore)

Romance Blossoms over the Ocean

In 2011, he returned to Hong Kong again to earn money. He worked at Physical Fitness as a dance teacher. One of his students, a Hong Kong lady named Fanny, caught his eye; the two began dating.

But making films was an addiction. He made his second film, a horror movie called *Bhoo*, in Hong Kong. He did it at the same time as his dance classes. It was exhausting. Making the film used up all his savings – HK$250,000. "Fanny told me not to invest my own money. She is not really into movies but understands and supports me." She is an accountant.

The two married in Hong Kong in January 2015. Her parents attended, but not his. "Fanny's family has welcomed me. We visit them on birthdays and at Chinese New Year. My father-in-law offers me whiskey and calls me 'A-Win' and says that I am a winner." He later brought his parents from India to meet his wife and her family.

The couple has visited Hyderabad together. "She likes the city and enjoys the shopping there." They have a son; his name is Vishwa Virat. Mother speaks to him in Cantonese, Father in English and Telugu. The young boy also learns Indian music online. Kishore continued his work as a music teacher.

In 2017, he flew back to Hyderabad for two months to make his third film, *Devi Sri Prasad*, an action movie. For this, he received a fee of HK$40,000. It was a commercial success.

Make a Film in Hong Kong?

The flying between Hyderabad and Hong Kong was exhausting. Friends suggested that he should make a film in Hong Kong. "I thought it would be too hard and too expensive. I had no Cantonese contacts. Why would anyone want to see my film, when there are so many film-makers here?"

So the idea came to his mind to do a Bollywood film, which local directors could not make. He wrote the story on and off from 2015 to 2017.

Raising the HK$3 million needed was an enormous challenge. "People said that you do not speak Cantonese nor write Chinese. They gave me one appointment, but not a second. Being an Indian is not easy. I needed to make people believe in me first, the concept after. I talked to everyone. I was talking, talking, talking."

Finally, he found Chinese investors willing to put in money; he could start preparing to shoot.

Photo above – Sri Kishore directing the actors. Below – With the production team and actors of *My Indian Boyfriend*. (© Sri Kishore)

"Through this film, I want to introduce Hong Kong actors to the Indian market and vice versa. It could be the way forward for Hong Kong cinema."

My Indian Boyfriend

The plot features Krishna, an idle Indian boy who falls in love with his neighbour Jasmine, an independent Hong Kong lady. Krishna is played by Karan Cholia, a local-born Indian who speaks fluent Cantonese. Jasmine is played by Shirley Chan, a well-known Hong Kong actress.

Her mother wants her to marry a wealthy and racist Hong Kong man. The father of Krishna prefers him to focus on making money. "I wanted a conflict that everyone would feel connected to. It is a romantic comedy. We went easy on the politics." He went to India to recruit 10 members of the crew and added 25 from Hong Kong.

"The story is perhaps two per cent inspired by my own love story. I am lucky that my wife is Hong Kong Chinese, so I have first-hand experience observing how our families interact."

Since it is a Bollywood film, song and dance are very important. There are seven song-and-dance sequences in the film, including 55 people performing on Chater Road in Central. The street protests caused a postponement of the shooting. Then COVID-19 arrived.

They finally did the shooting during 30 days in July and August 2020. Some locations required the permission of the police and the fire service. Shooting on public roads is allowed provided that it does not disturb traffic or the public.

"So we shot in the early morning, with few cars or people. We learnt certain tricks to deal with the police. Speak English with a strong foreign accent. They think you are a foreigner and are too troublesome. So they leave you alone. Most police do not speak English well. Also, many people do not dare to talk to foreigners."

During the filming, they used Hindi, Telugu, English and Cantonese.

In December 2020, he returned to Hyderabad for more shooting and a month of post-production work. On January 3, 2021, he returned to Hong Kong and served 21 days of quarantine. In February, he showed the film to a Hong Kong cinema company, which accepted it.

The Cantonese version was released on May 27, with 80 shows per days over five weeks. Well covered in Hong Kong media, it was a commercial success. Dubbed versions of the film in Hindi, Telugu and Tamil were due to be released in Malaysia, Singapore and India.

"It was a fruitful experience for Hong Kong and Indian cinema through the mixture of the cultures in the best way. Through this film, I wanted to introduce Hong Kong actors to the Indian market and vice versa. It could be the way forward for Hong Kong cinema."

Buddha in Hong Kong

Throughout this period, he was teaching Indian dance for 10 hours a week. Fortunately, his employer allowed him to take time off to make films.

"Now my body is weaker. I would prefer to teach about two hours a week and be a full-time film director. I have written a crime comedy thriller entitled *Buddha in Hong Kong*. My films do not deal with politics, but crime, love and human stories.

"Local film-making will only happen when passionate film-makers do it. Pakistanis and Indians here have many stories to tell. I have many stories to tell."

Towards Hong Kong, he has mixed feelings. "It is a good place, but people should be more open. I have had no support from the Indian community. I rarely meet Indians. I belong to the Chinese community – my wife and her family, my students and my friends."

Looking further ahead, he and his family might move to Hyderabad. "It is less expensive and more flexible."

15

German Actor Aims to Bring the World Together Through Film

Julian Gaertner

The moment that changed the life of Julian Gaertner came one summer day in 2006. He was with a friend in Hamburg on a cruise liner, which was making a one-night tour of the Norwegian coast, to go fishing and see nature.

"I saw a group of Chinese playing cards on the ship," he said. "They were intense and joyful, nibbling melon seeds and telling jokes. I had never seen Chinese so free and happy. Before, they had been formal and stoic. It made me ask the question: 'Are we humans all the same?'"

The experience persuaded him to come to China, learn both Cantonese and Mandarin, and find out what made the card-players laugh and cry.

Now, 15 years later, Gaertner lives in a three-storey villa on Peng Chau which he rents and hopes to buy. He has become the most famous foreign actor in the Cantonese film industry. He has played a Cantonese-speaking emperor and a ghost, as well as standard *gweilo* parts like a drunk, malevolent policeman.

He has the poetic name of 易宇航 (Yi You-hang) – the Astronaut Mr Yi. Yi is not a common surname. As far as anyone knows, there is only one Chinese out of 1.4 billion and no foreigner who shares this beautiful name. He was given it by a lady teacher of Mandarin in Shenzhen in 2009 – her name was 魚 (yu), fish, another essential part of the natural order. Yi is also the first character of 易經 (*Yi Jing*), *The Book of Changes*.

Playing Peer Gynt

There was little in Gaertner's childhood that pointed to such a destiny. He was born on December 8, 1987, one of four children of an Ear, Nose and Throat (ENT) doctor, in Munich, capital of Bavaria. His father managed the Gaertnerklinik, a 30-bed private clinic established by Julian's grandfather in the 1960s.

His parents were liberal and open-minded. They sent him to the private Waldorf School, where he took eight subjects for the German

Abitur, the equivalent of British A Levels.

"It was an all-round school, with social, farm, environmental and wood-making projects, in addition to the studies." A keen sportsman, he especially liked soccer.

His greatest love was acting. He played the title role of *Peer Gynt*, a romantic play by Norwegian Henrik Ibsen first performed in 1876. The school acting troupe went on tours in Germany.

"My parents did not force me, they let me do what I wanted. At 16, a conversation with a friend persuaded me to become serious with my studies and not merely be 'cool'. I was bad at mathematics and disliked it; but I caught up and came to like it. I was responsible for my life."

In 2004, he saw *2046*, a romantic film by Hong Kong director Wong Kar-wai. He also saw films starring Bruce Lee and Jackie Chan. All these encouraged him on the road toward becoming an actor.

In 2006, to improve his English, he went to live with a host family in San Diego, California for six months. "It was an exchange programme with a school. I learnt English fast. For a German, it is easy – not like Chinese."

His "awakening" on the cruise ship persuaded him to attend three month-long summer courses at Shenzhen University from 2006 to 2008, to learn Mandarin. He also attended courses at the University of Hong Kong (HKU).

Did his father ask him to study medicine and take over the family clinic? "When I was young, I worked there. I found it too predictable. My father was liberal. He allowed me to learn Chinese and Chinese medicine and go to HKU. The medical course is seven years long. My sister became a doctor and works at the clinic."

In 2007, he moved to HKU to study Political Science, Journalism and Geography. He received the Rosita King Ho Scholarship and HKU Worldwide Undergraduate Student Exchange Scholarship.

"The choice was whether to take the economic route and become an economic guy working for JP Morgan, or the art route. In this route, you might fall down and not survive."

Learning Cantonese

While many foreigners learn Mandarin, few learn Cantonese. So, what persuaded Julian to take the plunge?

"In any place you live, you want to speak the local language. It is magic to speak directly to people. Most of the students in my university dormitory were Hong Kong people. I wanted to belong and be accepted. On the soccer and lacrosse fields, everyone shouted in Cantonese."

He created his own romanisation system, based on German sounds. He also attended classes at HKU for mainland students who were learning Cantonese. "Many mainlanders learnt it, more quickly than I. When you talk to chefs, waiters and taxi drivers, you have a much deeper connection."

This knowledge has proved critical to his success in the Hong Kong film industry, especially at TV Broadcasts (TVB).

"On the film set, everyone speaks Cantonese. You find adapted English words, like 'mon' for monitor. Speaking Cantonese makes everyone enjoy what they are doing and not be nervous. You get the vibe in the room."

Shanghai Expo

In 2009 and 2010, his career could have taken a different path. From January 2009, he worked as an intern at the German Consulate-General in Shanghai. He put on a business suit and represented the consul at diplomatic functions. He wrote articles for its newsletter, wrote speeches for senior staff and helped to organise external events.

He also helped the consulate prepare for the World Expo, held in the city the next year. Between February and September 2010, he worked with a production company to develop, host and present a multi-lingual and interactive show, "The Energy Source" for the German pavilion. It was seen by 20,000 people a day for its six-month run. Julian acted as host and presenter. The pavilion won the prize for "Best in Show".

He could have kept wearing the business suit and become a diplomat or consultant. But he did not.

Start-up

Julian graduated from HKU in 2012 with a Bachelor's degree. Then he established a start-up, Live It China Limited, of which he was CEO. It was a free and open social media platform for Chinese language learning that enabled users to share their learning experiences. It guided users through the whole learning process from start to finish. He ran the company for four years, before selling it in 2015.

From 2011, he was a part-time actor, fitting it in between study and work. From March 2010 to March 2011, he was co-host of *Angel's World*, a weekly children's television show in Cantonese on ATV. It introduced different cultures, food and cultural habits in an entertaining way.

In 2015, he became a full-time actor at TVB. He started with *gweilo* roles, such as a policeman who drank a lot and misbehaved toward Chinese women. Then his roles improved, including playing Chinese characters. His knowledge of Cantonese was essential; all the scripts were in Chinese.

"At TVB, the pace of production is very fast. It is a very traditional company, with no rules and no unions. You must do it their way. I have learnt a lot there and made mistakes. I earned advertisement deals."

His roles included: a foreign ambassador; an evil American sailor who befriends two Chinese families in *Bangkok Chinatown*; and a ghost in *The Exorcist's 2nd Meter* he plays a demon who comes from an ancient counterfeit painting.

This was his most famous role in Hong Kong and has earned

Photo above – Julian Gaertner plays a British police inspector in *Chasing the Dragon*. Below – In *The Exorcist's Meter 2.0*, Gaertner plays Billy. (© Julian Gaertner)

him fan mail from the city, the mainland and Canada. "I like to communicate with my fans. This is the uniqueness of Hong Kong, a city of many languages and different cultures."

Mountain-top Home

From 2011 to 2016, Julian lived in cramped apartments in Aberdeen and Kennedy Town. In 2016, he moved to a three-storey house with six rooms on the top of a hill in the island of Peng Chau. It has no cars.

"I pay HK$10,000 a month in rent and would like to buy it. That would cost HK$3-4 million. I have a good relationship with the landlord, who teaches me Chinese philosophy, including Zhuangzi."

The house is equipped with computers, film and editing equipment, so that Julian can work there. He enjoys the peace and quiet of the island, explores it on foot or on his bicycle, and swims on its beaches.

The only downside is the journey of 90 minutes to the TVB studio in Tseung Kwan O. "But often they are shooting somewhere in the city, which is a shorter journey."

After stops and starts, he has started a long-term relationship with a Hong Kong lady, who can understand and support his vision. Together they share places now in Peng Chau and Central.

Links to Germany

He remains in close contact with his family in Munich. "Several years ago, Father had one of his heart valves replaced. This has caused problems. In 2020, he had a tweak in his heart. I was worried and went back to see him. He is better now. I took over some of his tasks."

His father, 69 in 2021, is semi-retired but continues to work at his clinic, as a manager and developing new therapies. He has changed its status to a foundation owned by the government. In a conservative

"In any place you live, you want to speak the local language. It is magic to speak directly to people. I wanted to belong and be accepted."

profession, he is open-minded.

In 2020, Julian introduced a Chinese doctor who had studied traditional Chinese medicine in Sichuan and then ENT medicine in Germany. His father hired him as an employee at the clinic; it now offers acupuncture and other traditional treatments. The clinic also offers music therapy and free treatment for addiction to mobile telephones.

"Father sees illness coming from stress, lifestyle choice and bad relationships. He takes an inter-disciplinary approach. I encourage him – but this raises difficulties with other doctors and insurance companies. They say these new treatments are not science-based.

"My sister is more conservative, after studying for seven years in Germany to become a doctor. She and Father often misunderstand each other and I act as mediator."

Hold the World Together

Looking ahead, Julian wants to keep Hong Kong and his house in Peng Chau as his base. "An actor should not have only one home. He should go to new places."

He would like to make his own films. To this end, he is setting up a company with money from European funds based in Hong Kong and Salon Films and is applying for a grant from the Hong Kong government.

"We have producers in Macao, the mainland, Hong Kong and Germany. But the pandemic has delayed projects."

He has written an eight-part martial arts film, with each episode of one hour. "The main character wakes up during his past lives."

"As an actor and producer myself, I can realise the full extent of my artistic value."

In addition, in 2021, he launched a new App "Find Your Language Partner", to help people learn Chinese and English.

He is concerned about possible restrictions on art and culture in

Hong Kong. "Of course, pure nudity and populism must be restricted. But, if art is dull, that defeats its purpose. How can you be innovative?

"Hong Kong's role is to be creative and work in many languages, in film, advertising, global relations, culture and philosophy. People here can make all this accessible.

"I want to tell stories and bring people together so that they become friends. Art and films inspire many people and can hold the world together. This is very important. We are a bridge. Is it not the greatest privilege to bring cultures together through entertainment?"

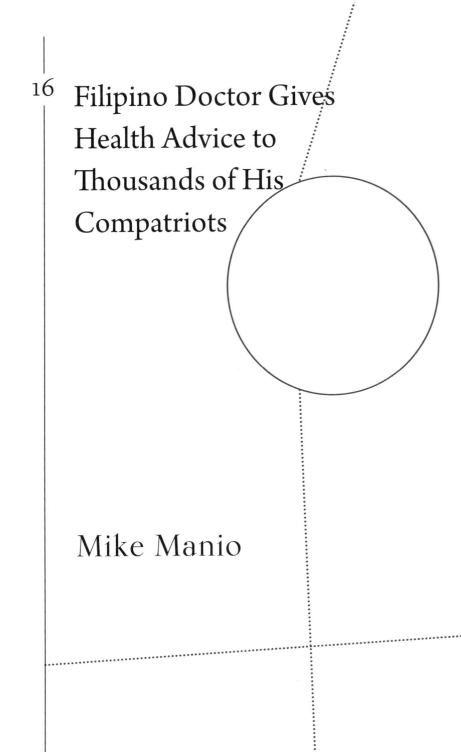

16 Filipino Doctor Gives Health Advice to Thousands of His Compatriots

Mike Manio

Doctor Mike Manio arrived in Hong Kong on August 29, 2010, a Sunday. He saw hundreds of women sitting on pieces of cardboard on the street in the summer heat – and slowly realised they were his Filipino compatriots.

In the years since, he has devoted his time and energy to helping them. He organised classes on health, nutrition and workers' rights and now provides health advice at a Kowloon clinic and online that reaches 30,000 Filipinos in Hong Kong, Indonesia, Singapore, Kuwait and Saudi Arabia.

"I believe God sent me here with a purpose, to help the domestic workers. Before I came, my plan was to study and be my best. But Hong Kong opened the door for me. It has developed my education, career and social skills. I hope that people I teach will treat their maids better."

Volcano and Typhoons

Manio was born on May 8, 1977, the elder of two sons of a middle-class family in Pampanga Province, 70 kilometres from the capital Manila in the central island of Luzon.

His father worked as a seaman on an international cargo ship from 1974 until early 2000. During that time, he spent only two-to-three months of every year at home. "In my childhood, there was no Internet. We had to take a jeepney to a place where my father would make a call from the ship.

"My mother was both father and mother. She hired a private tutor to complement what we learnt at school. She told us we needed to excel. If we passed an exam and received an award, she would reward us. Father did not like to work abroad. Each time he left, he and mother cried."

On June 16, 1991, nearby Mount Pinatubo erupted, pouring lahar over the surrounding areas. It was the second largest terrestrial eruption of the 20th century after the 1912 eruption of Novarupta in

Alaska. Half of the Manio home was covered in lahar, so the family had to rent another house one hour away; Mike had to move to another school. "In addition, several typhoons strike the Philippines each year. They left one metre of flood water in our two-storey home. So, we had to keep our important items on the second floor. But my parents loved the area and refused to move elsewhere."

Initially, Manio wanted to train as a lawyer. But his parents opposed this, on the grounds that many lawyers were targets of assassinations in a country where many disputes are settled by guns.

So, they persuaded him to become a doctor instead. During his school years, Manio eagerly took part in extra-curricular activities such as dance, singing and drama. In 1998, he was President of the School Council and went to the country's Senate, where he met many political leaders.

Four-Hour Commute to Class

The journey to qualification was long and exhausting. In 1998, he began his medical studies at the Angeles University one-and-a-half hours away from his home. In 2005, after completing his medical studies and training at Holy Angel University, he became a full-time Assistant Professor in the nursing school.

In addition, he enrolled at the University of Santo Tomas (UST) in Manila. This involved a four-hour return bus journey three days a week, from Pampanga to Manila for a three-hour class at 6pm and returning home after the class. In May 2008, he graduated cum laude from UST with a Master of Health Professions Education.

Then he was awarded a Presidential Scholarship to the University of the Philippines (UP) to continue his post-graduate medical studies. While he was there, he learnt that a professor from the University of Hong Kong (HKU) was seeking graduate students.

Aware of the fame of HKU, he applied for and received a scholarship to prepare for a doctorate in Medicine. It was the summer of 2010. "I had zero knowledge of Hong Kong, outside Disneyland and Ocean Park."

Cardboard People

On August 29, 2010, Manio arrived at Chep Lap Kok airport, with HK$2,000 in his pocket. He was met by a female former student who was also cousin of a colleague at Holy Angel University. Unable to find work at home, she had become a domestic worker in Hong Kong.

It was the worst moment to be a Filipino in Hong Kong. Six days previously, police in Manila had stormed a tourist bus with 22 Hong Kong people on board; they had been kidnapped by a former policeman who was heavily armed.

During the gun-battle that lasted 60 minutes, the kidnapper and eight Hong Kongers were killed. People in Hong Kong considered that the police had bungled the operation and held the Philippine government responsible.

As Manio and his friend drove through Central, they saw people protesting against his government. "If anyone asked me, I said I was Mexican, Thai or Malaysian – anything but Filipino."

The other thing that caught his eye was hundreds of young women sitting on pieces of cardboard on the streets in the sweltering heat. "Who were they? Street sleepers" I asked myself. His friend said: "No, these are Filipino domestic workers on their only day off during the week. If they stay at home, their employers will give them work to do. So, they have to go outside – and sitting on the street costs nothing."

He went to Ricci Hall, the Jesuit residential hall attached to HKU; he would stay there for two years. The first months were difficult. He had no idea the cost of living was so high and he was short of money; he had no credit card. "For free meals, I went to conferences and seminars.

"I knew no-one. Everyone asked me if I was a driver or domestic

Mike Manio in front of Hong Kong University. (© Mike Manio)

worker. I was hurt. In our laboratory, no-one invited me out for lunch. I had it on my own. My former student invited me to bars and night clubs in Central and Wan Chai. I did not want to go. I was afraid I would be arrested by the police and disgrace the name of HKU."

Then a colleague introduced him to Filipino doctors working for three months at Queen Mary Hospital. They became his friends for meals and hiking on weekends.

He settled down. He found the studies at HKU very productive; he graduated in 2014. The Dean of Student Affairs hired him on a one-year contract to teach students how to work in the wider community.

In 2012, he won an award in a research competition. This caught the attention of the Philippine Consul-General who invited him to give talks on health issues to the Filipino community on Sundays at the consulate; it started with 30-40 in the audience.

Empowerment

This was the start of a project that would take up much of the next five years. He spent many Sundays on the streets, talking to and teaching the maids. He found among them a hunger for learning and self-improvement. Many were well educated, including university graduates; but lack of jobs at home had forced them to became foreign workers.

In November 2014, he set up the Domestic Workers Empowerment Projects (DWEP) to give them lessons on practical health and nutrition, basic rights and empowerment, nature appreciation, physical fitness and performing art. "Our aim was to upgrade their knowledge and skills, help them assimilate to life in HK and help prepare for life after."

Since space at the consulate was limited, he asked HKU if they could use its classrooms. "They were sceptical at the start and said that the ladies were not paying students. Opening the rooms on Sunday meant security, additional staff and other costs."

Then the university relented and agreed to let its classrooms be used. The demand was enormous, up to 600 for some lectures. Manio invited his university colleagues to speak about their specialties. The main subjects were health and wellness and workers' rights.

"The domestic workers wept when they entered the campus. It was the first time in their lives that they had come to HKU. It showed that it is not only for the rich and the elite. Some said that their employers were HKU graduates and would look at them differently after the classes."

But funding was always a problem. The university paid him just HK$12,000 a month for the programme. He had to rely on individual and corporate donors. The courses continued until the end of 2019, when the street protests made physical classes impossible.

Mike Manio cares for the Filipina domestic maids of Hong Kong. During the weekends, he often goes to see them. (© Mike Manio)

Clinic, Online and Offline

In August 2020, he stepped down from DWEP. "Two colleagues opened a clinic here (in Chatham Road North) and invited me to join them. I decided that I could help my compatriots more on the medical side."

The All Grace Medical and Well Personal Clinic opened in August 2020 and largely serves Filipino migrant workers; they account for 70 per cent of the patients. Of the rest, 20 per cent are Chinese and 10 per cent Filipino residents.

It offers its first consultation free of charge, with HK$200 for the second. The other two doctors are Chinese. "Since we opened, we have had 2,000 patients, mostly at the weekends. I focus on health teaching and preventive health, which is very important."

Since February 2020, Manio has also become very active on

YouTube and Facebook, aiming at Filipino domestic workers not only in Hong Kong but all over the world. "I have 30,000 followers on both media, with some in Kuwait, Saudi Arabia, Singapore, Indonesia and the U.K. We have content in English and Tagalog. We have commercials to provide funding."

Plight of the Workers

"The workers pay a heavy price for the life they have chosen in Hong Kong. If there were opportunities at home, they would not come," Manio said. "They do it because they want an education for their children. "But, of those who come, nearly half lose their marriage because of the separation. Their families become dysfunctional. They care for the children of their host family but not their own. If they are not caring for children, they are looking after dogs or cats."

The irregular visits mean that the family cannot stay together. In the Philippines, a country where the Catholic church holds enormous power, divorce is illegal – so the women cannot marry a second time.

Most contracts allow for a home visit every two years; in some cases, it is four-to-six years. What makes it worse is the debt they owe to the recruiting agent when they arrive. Frequent home visits would only increase this debt.

"I feel their pain. My father worked overseas for most of his life. Some speak to me of their mental anguish."

But the poor state of the Philippine economy and high unemployment mean that more and more people want to work abroad.

"Hong Kong is the most attractive option, better than Saudi Arabia and Gulf countries. It is closest and easiest and less dangerous. There they may be abused or raped. All these factors mean that many do not wish to return home, because they cannot find work or set up a business there.

"Some came in their 30s and have stayed for 30 years. One retired to the Philippines and then married a friend from her childhood. She

Mike Manio takes a group of Filipina maids to Tap Mun, to help them understand Hong Kong life and culture. (© Mike Manio)

was 62. One good employer bought a house in the Philippines for his maid when she retired.

"There should be an integration programme. They should not wait for 20-to-30 years, when it will be too late to rebuild their family. I tell them to save money, develop skills they can use at home and prepare for a future with their family."

Celibate

For the last 11 years, Manio has lived among thousands of young Filipina ladies, holding a prestigious professional job – a highly desirable partner. But he remains celibate.

"A professional needs to set boundaries. I have always kept this

"Hong Kong is my second home. I have made many friends and contributed to Hong Kong and Filipino people."

boundary. A majority of the migrant workers are married, with families in the Philippines. I need to think of my core values." He is a devout Catholic.

He plans to stay a further 10 years in Hong Kong. "Before, I used to say I would stay three-to-four years. But I impart knowledge now and want to continue what I do. Hong Kong is my second home. I have made many friends and contributed to Hong Kong and Filipino people." He lives in an apartment of 600 square feet. "I have no maid. The apartment is too small, I clean it myself."

His parents are open-minded and are not asking him to come home. They leave him to decide. His younger brother is Asia/Pacific manager for a food company and lives in the Philippines; he has three children.

When he finally leaves, he could return to the Philippines or Canada or the United States, where he has relatives. Manio sees the trials he has endured in his life as a form of training. "When I arrived in Hong Kong, I became angry when people insulted me. But I did not argue with them. I wanted people with positive energy.

"When I was in primary and secondary school in the Philippines, I was bullied and insulted by the other students. This gave me strength and determination to do my best. In 2019, I returned to the school to receive an award as its 'most successful alumnus'. The audience included those who beat me. I publicly thanked them in my speech of acceptance."

Chapter. 3

IN THE NAME
OF
LOVE

Brother Thomas
Lavin

Brother Thomas Lavin began teaching at La Salle College in Kowloon on 1st September 1965. Over the last 56 years, he has served as teacher, sports master, principal and Supervisor. He has taught thousands of students – they live in Hong Kong and scattered around the world.

The school will celebrate its 90th anniversary in January 2022. It will be an occasion for them to pay tribute to him and the other Irish brothers who have devoted their lives to educating them. The school transformed their lives, giving education, skills and English fluency that opened to them careers here and in many countries.

Each year Thomas visits his family and fellow La Salle Brothers in his native Ireland but does not want to live there. "I do not wish to retire in Ireland. Hong Kong is my home."

In addition to Hong Kong, he has worked in Nigeria, the Holy Land and Malaysia.

Thomas was born on June 16, 1943, in Ballaghaderreen, a town of around 1,000 people in Co Roscommon in the west of Ireland. He is the eldest of four children. His father worked in a hardware store and, for the last 15 years of his working life, as a porter in the local bank, which gave him a pension.

"Fortunately, my father was a very hard-working family man. A teetotaler – known in Ireland as a 'pioneer' – he never drank, and he was employed in our town throughout his life. He and my mum took great care of us. We had a garden where we grew potatoes and vegetables. In the 1950s in Ireland, no-one was well-off, but we were comfortable." The family rented a bog outside the town; the children went there with Dad to cut the peat they used as fuel for heating and cooking.

His parents were devout Catholics, with his father attending Mass every day and saying the Rosary after the family dinner every evening.

The small town offered few job opportunities to its young people but was blessed with fine schools managed by religious orders.

Thomas attended the Primary School run by the La Salle

Brothers, a religious order founded in France in 1680 and devoted to education.

During his final year at the school, Thomas heard a talk by a La Salle Brother sent to inform the students about joining the order. "I was excited by the talk and decided to enroll." He was just 14. Later one of his brothers also decided to become a priest. His parents were delighted.

"In the 1950s, the majority of students emigrated. There was very little work around the town. Joining a religious order was a very good choice. To be a priest, Brother or Sister was prestigious, going up in the social order. It meant that you would receive a good education."

So began the start of an eight-year educational odyssey before he left for Hong Kong. He spent the first two years at a boarding school run by the La Salle Brothers in Mallow, Co Cork in the south of Ireland. Then followed two years at another La Salle Centre in Castletown, Co Laois.

"Many dropped out because they were homesick, could not accept celibacy or found the life of a Brother did not suit them. But such doubts never bothered me much. I think this is the gift of 'being called' and I thank God for it."

Near the end of the Novitiate when Thomas was 17, he was asked to make a momentous decision. Did he wish to stay in Ireland or be sent to work on the mission in the Far East meaning Malaysia, Singapore, or Hong Kong. "I was excited by mission work, so I volunteered." Five Brothers from our group of 26 were chosen.

Then he spent five years doing O and A Levels and teacher's training in England. "At the first place, near Newbury in Berkshire in the southeast of England, some of the young English Brothers teased us for our thick Irish accents but we didn't mind. Much more important was that the food was plentiful and fabulous, especially the desserts. In the Irish training schools, I remember being hungry most of the time."

He spent three years at De La Salle Teacher Training College in Manchester. He studied English Literature as his major subject. He also developed a love of sports, especially soccer and Manchester United. The Brother Principal of the College was a friend of Matt Busby, the team's manager, and had tickets for big matches at Old Trafford, home of United. He would give them to the young Brothers from time to time. Thomas was able to go there and watch fellow Irishman George Best, one of the greatest players of his era.

By the end of his training, the five who had chosen a mission in the Far East had become two. "Our director told us we were going to Hong Kong. I only knew vaguely where it was. There was no preparation, in terms of language or culture training, as there is now."

The plane journey from London in August 1965 required five stops. He remembers getting out at every stop as the plane was refuelling. Thomas was assigned to La Salle College and found himself living on the first floor of the La Salle College in a community of 12 brothers. It was a disciplined life, with regular prayer time, school classes and a common room where they corrected the work of the students. He was just 22.

He was given the task of teaching English, religious studies and mathematics to Form 1, the 12-year-olds. One of his students was Peter Wong Tung-shun, who would go on to become Group General Manager of HSBC for many years. He soon realised that he had to learn to speak slowly and learn how to pronounce the Chinese names of his students.

On 13th December 1968, aged 25, Thomas made his final profession. This meant that he undertook to stay with the Order for the rest of his life. "I had no doubt that this was the right way of life for me."

He taught for four years at La Salle. Then, in 1969, he went as a mature student to University College, Dublin to take a bachelor's degree in Economics. His results were so good that he won a scholarship and stayed a fourth year for a master's degree, graduating with honours in 1973.

He returned to La Salle College for a further nine years during which he was given heavier responsibilities, teaching Form 6 and 7 who were preparing for A Levels. His main subject was economics. He was also heavily involved in activities outside class, especially sports.

In the mid-1970s, the school faced a critical decision – whether or not to demolish the original building completed in 1932 and build a new campus. Brother Raphael Egan, the principal, believed the building was inadequate and needed to be demolished. Mr. Li Ka-shing, chairman of Cheung Kong (CK) asked for a third of the school plot in exchange for CK building a modern, state-of-the-art school on the same site.

"The community was very divided. The older brothers could not accept complete demolition. It was a very tough time. I met Mr. Li Ka-shing and was convinced that he genuinely wanted us to have a top-notch school campus and he would pay whatever it took. Eventually, after a lot of discussion, the community voted in favor of the proposal."

This meant that La Salle did not need to seek a penny of money from the government or its old boys for this re-development project.

The new school brought facilities they had never enjoyed before – a 400-metre running track, a 50-metre Olympic-size swimming pool, a gymnasium, an Astroturf football field, air conditioning through the whole building and modern science laboratories. The Brothers continued to live on the top floor of the new building. Thomas designed all the sports facilities – the track and field, swimming pool and indoor gymnasium.

On February 19, 1982, Governor Sir Murray MacLehose officiated at the ceremony to open the new campus. It was the Golden Anniversary year of the school.

"After five years engaged in the new school project, I was feeling tired and burnt out. So, I asked the Provincial (his superior) for a sabbatical." He went to the University of Manchester and earned a M.A. in Education. One bonus was to be able to go to Old Trafford again to see the home games of Manchester United. But this second time was even better because the La Salle community had a season ticket.

In the 1960s, Brother Thomas was sent to teach at La Salle College in Kowloon. (© La Salle College)

"During my year in Manchester, I was asking myself if I wanted to spend all my life at La Salle College? Maybe I should consider trying another mission before returning. So, when the Irish Provincial invited me to join the staff of a teacher training college run by the Irish Brothers in northern Nigeria, I accepted the offer. It was to be for one year."

Culture Shock

In February 1984, he arrived in Nigeria. The contrast with the orderly life in Hong Kong and spotless uniforms of Kowloon Tong could not have been sharper.

"It was a struggle to find fuel for our generators, clean water and vehicles that worked. We had five or six power cuts a day. Most teachers had other jobs. The roads were bad and the driving terrible. The biggest killer was road accidents. Two of our best local Brothers were killed in car crashes. Animals walked as they wished across the road. There was corruption everywhere. I contracted malaria several times. I was lucky to be alive."

What sustained him was the smiling optimism of the people despite all the difficulties they faced and the inspiration of John Baptist de La Salle, the Order's founder, who devoted his life to educating the poor and the needy.

After one year, Thomas accepted to become Rector of a Minor Seminary School in Yola which meant returning to Hong Kong was put on hold. He was now facing challenges unknown in Hong Kong schools – getting students and teachers to report on time, preparing a school timetable before schools opened and making teachers stick to it: ensuring honesty in the use of funds.

"Corporal punishment was overused by the teachers and the prefects. I forbade it and was not very popular with some staff. Our purpose was to create model schools for others to follow and to encourage local Brothers. Students responded to these improvements and the school was soon a leading school in the State."

After six years as Rector in the Minor Seminary, he was transferred to become Principal of the Brothers school near Makurdi in Benue State. This was his first time working in a co-ed school. He soon saw that the biggest challenge was persuading girl students to remain in class when they were often married young and became pregnant. After the birth, he allowed them to come back to school. This was much appreciated.

At the same time, he was elected Director of the La Salle Brothers in the whole of the country. This required frequent travel and exposed him to new, potentially fatal, dangers.

"I had a good driver, and we went everywhere together. All over the country, there were roadblocks where armed men extorted money. Priests and Sisters were sometimes robbed and killed on the roads."

The most frightening moment came when they were stopped at

The opening of the new school building. (© La Salle College)

a road block near the border with Cameroon. Armed men ordered him and the driver out of the car and walked them over a hill to a place where a dozen people were sitting with their faces looking to the ground. "We waited for an hour. We were terrified that we would be killed. After an hour, everything had fallen quiet. We got up and walked back to the car. The robbers had taken our bags, passports and everything else, but left the vehicle."

His main responsibility at this time was helping to create a new association of English-speaking Brothers in Africa. "We wanted to give them a sense of pan-Africanism and independence so as not to have to look to Europe or the USA all the time." This new association or "District" included Anglophone countries with Lasallian missions: Nigeria, South Africa, Kenya, Ethiopia, and Eritrea.

Each summer he returned to Ireland to see his family and have a medical check-up at the Tropical Centre in Our Lady of Lourdes Hospital Drogheda Co. Louth. He would also meet up most years with Brother Patrick Tierney from Hong Kong when he was on holiday. "He kept me up to date."

Principal of La Salle

Thomas returned to La Salle HK in September 1998 and decided to stay. He felt his work in Nigeria could now be taken over by the local Brothers. He began to help the Hong Kong Lasallian Family. When Brother Patrick finished his term as Principal in 2000, Thomas took over the post; he held it for four years.

"The big issue we were facing was whether we should join the Direct Subsidy System (DSS), which allowed aided schools to charge fees in addition to the Government grants they were receiving. We were under a lot of pressure to join but finally decided not to. Our tradition from our founder John Baptist de La Salle is that we should not charge fees and so be open to everyone, rich and poor alike. We wanted to be faithful to this."

He reached the retirement age in 2003 but applied for an extension for one year. This was approved, as there was no Brother to replace him and a layman would be appointed Principal for the first time. The Education Dept accepted that time was needed to select a layman and have the appointment approved.

The next two Principals, from 2004 to 2010, were laymen. In 2010, a De La Salle Brother from New Zealand, Brother Steve Hogan, took over; he held the post for six years.

The Holy Land

After one year as Supervisor, Thomas was invited in 2005 to go to the Holy Land to teach economics at the Lasallian University in Bethlehem. He would also work on the professional development of teachers. The community was made up of mainly American and Palestinian Brothers. "It was a wonderful experience. It was a very good community of university people, very hard-working. I would have loved to stay longer but had promised to come back after one year."

On Saturdays, he went to Jerusalem, just 10 kilometres away, through the Israeli West Bank wall. "Because it was the Jewish Sabbath, there was no traffic. So I was able to walk around the Old City and the holy places."

Because of the Intifada – the Palestinian rebellion – the campus was often closed but would then reopen and carry on as normal.

His students were Palestinians. "I lived in the West Bank and listened to talks there. I was very sympathetic to the Palestinians. The wall is so divisive. You see how well off the Israelis are, compared to the poverty of the Palestinians. Control of water is critical."

Brother Visitor of Penang District

In 2006, Thomas moved to Kuala Lumpur, capital of Malaysia, to become Provincial (Brother Visitor) of the Brothers in Malaysia, Singapore and Hong Kong, which was called the District of Penang. Much of his time was spent, as in Africa, in forming a new structure for the Brothers in East Asia.

In 2011, the District of Penang joined with the Philippines, Thailand, Burma, and Japan, to form a new entity of seven countries called the Lasallian East Asia District (LEAD). A Filipino Brother became the Brother Visitor, and he was appointed Auxiliary Visitor. Hong Kong was selected to be the headquarters, so he returned to live there. "It involved a great deal of travel, conferences and meetings." The LEAD Brothers are mostly Asian, with a small number of Europeans and three Mexicans in Japan.

Building an International School

Then, in 2015, he embarked on a new project – opening a Lasallian international school in Petaling Jaya in Selangor State in Malaysia.

St Joseph's Institution International School opened in August 2016, with 430 students. In 2021 it had more than 800 with more

"Doubts never bothered me much. I think this is the gift of 'being called' and I thank God for it. I had no doubt that this was the right way of life for me."

than 29 different nationalities. The majority are Malaysian Chinese, followed by Koreans and Japanese.

"The Brothers have been providing education in Malaysia since 1852. The La Salle name is very well known and is a strong selling point for the new school. So also, is our link to St. Joseph's Institution International Singapore which was opened in 2007.

"Of all my assignments, this was the toughest. I had no experience of international education. Our partner in Malaysia who gave the land and built the school was very 'commercial' and difficult to work with."

Brother Thomas had a three-year contract, which expired in 2018, so he returned to Hong Kong in summer 2018. Since then, he has been Supervisor of La Salle. "I have been lucky, my health has remained good."

Going Home?

Each year, if possible, Thomas returns to see his family in Ireland. His parents have passed away, so he visits his two brothers – one lives in Galway City and the other, who is a priest, has retired and lives in Knock, Co Mayo.

"I also like to spend time with the Brothers, especially those in our retirement home in Castletown, Co Laois. Usually, my holiday is about three weeks."

The Ireland of today bears little resemblance to the country of his childhood. Very few young men are training to be priests and the religious orders, including his own, are disappearing.

The La Salle Brothers no longer run the schools they set up. Independent trusts have been established to manage the schools; the Brothers have a role and can visit them to promote the ethos and encourage the students to become members, but they do not manage the schools anymore.

"The number of young men joining the priesthood and religious life has fallen drastically. After Vatican II (1962-65), many priests and

Dedicating his life to education.

religious left. The Irish economy improved greatly, and family sizes reduced. There was also a public reaction against clerical abuse of children and corporal punishment in the schools.

"Today countries like the Philippines and Nigeria are like Ireland in the 1950's and 60's – large families, limited job opportunities and high social status of priests and religious. The seminaries are bursting at the seams."

Since Brother Thomas joined the order in 1957, the world has changed beyond recognition. He could never have imagined the journey he would make, to many places around the world.

18

French Woman Falls in Love and Spends Life in Hong Kong

Paulette Yvonne
Octavie Lane

A week of frozen weather in the small town of Pitlochry in the north of Scotland in 1960 changed the destiny of a young French student. It was there that she met the Hong Kong man who became her husband.

On March 15, 1961, Paulette Yvonne Octavie Lane married her sweetheart, Tsoi Shiu Foo, James, at a civil office in London. Only six people attended the ceremony, none of them relatives. Paulette's family did not approve of the marriage and James' family was not even aware of it.

On August 23, 1962, she arrived in Hong Kong on the M.V "Asia", an Italian passenger boat, to be met by about 30 members of the Tsoi family. It was the first time she had left Europe. "It was total shock," she said. She did not speak a word of Cantonese.

Since then she has spent 59 years in Hong Kong, except for holidays and short stays in France with her family and later with her husband.

Growing up

Paulette was born on July 16, 1939 in the commune of Eu in Normandy, northern France. Her mother, from Douai in the north of France, had been appointed as a teacher there. Her father was a policeman. He had to join the army and was captured by the Germans at Dunkirk in 1940. He spent the next five years as a worker in Germany. He initially was put in a camp in Bohemia, and the internees worked in the farms nearby. A few months later, he was transferred to a farm further north.

The son of that family had also gone to war. His parents hoped he would return safely and that people would be kind to him, so they treated Paulette's father well. Then he was transferred to Kiel, a port on the Baltic Sea where he worked as a nurse. In the closing days of the war, American and Soviet troops each rushed to occupy as much of Germany as possible.

He and his colleagues escaped and walked on foot to the Czech capital of Prague, a distance of 560 kilometres. There he met British and American soldiers; they repatriated him to Douai, where his wife lived with her parents and Paulette.

"I was six and had never seen him. I was afraid," said Paulette. "I hid between a wardrobe and the wall and did not want to come out. My mother had to entice me out with a piece of chocolate, so that he could embrace the daughter he had not seen for more than five years."

Paulette and her mother spent the war partly with her maternal grandmother in Douai and partly with her paternal grandmother in Crecques, a small village near Aire-sur-la-Lys in the Pas de Calais. The whole of northern France was occupied by the Germans.

In her paternal grandmother's village, below the hills of Artois, the Germans had installed V1 (missile, or flying bomb) launching ramps. Each house in the village had a resident German soldier watching the family.

Yet her grandmother, who lived in an isolated house, managed to hide a British parachutist in a pigeon coop in her barn where the Germans would not find him; later on, she escorted him through streams, to safety.

Paulette did not attend school during the war but benefited from the excellent tuition of her mother; by the time she was four, she could read and write. After the end of the war, normal education resumed. Paulette flourished: "I wanted to be a teacher like my mother, get a good salary, long holidays and retirement at 55".

In 1957, she went a lycee in Paris to study for the entrance exam to École Normale Supérieure. But, although she did well, she realised she did not want to join that School. So, she went back to the North to the University of Lille, where she studied English and Spanish.

The course included one year of study in England, arranged by the university. Students were assigned to a grammar school and given conversation lessons. She was assigned to the Frimley and Camberley Grammar School in Camberley, home of the Royal Military Academy

Sandhurst. Paulette stayed in a house owned by Ms Flora Flower, who was single; it was a large house which she could no longer maintain. So, she would take lodgers, usually three of them, and Paulette joined what was in fact a "family unit" – everybody got on very well.

Flora and her nephew, Major Robert Clutterbuck, an instructor at Sandhurst, took it to heart to improve her English; she was not allowed to use wrong words or expressions and was always corrected for her mistakes. After eight months, Paulette could speak excellent English.

At Christmas, in 1960, Paulette returned to France for the holidays. Paulette had grown up with Jean Claude, whose mother was a friend of her mother; both mothers hoped that their children would marry.

Jean Claude was a student of chemistry at Strasbourg, in the east of the country. In fact, Paulette was feeling a little homesick and welcomed the idea of marrying Jean Claude; it was even suggested that they could marry in June 1961.

Forbidden Romance

Paulette returned to England after the Christmas holidays. The headmaster of the school was Scottish and keen for Paulette to "discover" Scotland. The British Council was offering a one-week stay in February in an old manor on the shore of a loch in Pitlochry, a pretty tourist town in Perthshire, in the heart of Scotland.

The manor had been left to the students of the University of Aberdeen by an eccentric Scotsman who had lived there for years all alone; the students were to be hosts to students who would join the programme offered by the British Council.

Part of Paulette's trip was sponsored by her school; but, to save money, Paulette hitch-hiked all the way to Scotland which was rare in those days. Paulette says she only met kindness on the way. One of her "drivers" was concerned about her and drove her to the police station in York, so that they could find safe overnight accommodation. She ended up staying with the family of one of the policemen; early the next morning, he took her and his daughter to visit York Cathedral.

At the Manor, there were about 20 students – several from the Netherlands, one French, one German, one Indian, four Japanese and one Hong Kong Chinese, Tsoi Shiu Foo also known as James. He was finishing his studies at Imperial College in London. He had entered university late because he had not been able to receive tertiary education in Hong Kong during the war. The Japanese had invaded Hong Kong in 1941 and occupied it until August 1945. He was 10 years older than she.

In February in Scotland, it was freezing cold. "The manor was a very attractive place, a large estate along the loch and the river with huge trees. Inside the main room which had served in the old days as a ballroom, there was a huge stone fireplace, where half a tree-trunk would burn... It was a focus place for meeting. Everyone got on well. Together we danced, drank whiskey and tried haggis and made local visits. The people from the small town came and played bag-pipes. It was quite an experience.

"At first, James and I were not particularly attracted... but he was always one of the last ones, sitting in front of the fire place, to leave. And so we talked quite a bit. At night, I loved to walk alone along the loch – it was very safe – and I found out that he was doing the same, and so we walked together. We discovered that we had in fact much in common. He had not seen his family for years because in those days it was not easy to travel and quite expensive and students tended to stay in England for the duration of their studies. He was finishing his studies and was to begin work with Costain, a well-known construction company in England; he was hoping to gain experience and obtain his professional qualification as a civil engineer. Then he would return to Hong Kong and work there.

Six of them travelled in the train together back to London. Paulette finished her academic year at Camberley and registered to finish her last year at the University of Lille, in conjunction with the

French Lycee in London which had an arrangement with the Lille University.

She also worked as a French teacher at a private Catholic school in Woldingham in Surrey. She moved to the "Residence" in Maida Vale where James and many of his friends lived. She shared a room with a Burmese lady, who was studying for a special postgraduate diploma in Tropical Diseases. The relationship between James and Paulette flourished.

At Easter, Paulette went back to her family in France. Although marriage had not been mentioned between James and Paulette, she knew she could not marry Jean Claude. The conversation with her mother is not something Paulette likes to remember. She was basically thrown out of the house and returned to London before the end of the Easter Holidays.

Having married James in March 1961, Paulette decided to mend her relations with her family; they both travelled to the North of France in July. Everyone was making an effort. James did not speak a single word of French; apart from Paulette's paternal grandfather who was English, no one spoke that language. But it was touching to see how he tried to fit in; her family realised that and "took him in".

"So, my family liked him and accepted him. He helped my uncle to fit a very old radio which he had kept from the war; it was on that radio that Uncle would listen to the messages of General de Gaulle during the war. The radio was completely broken, but together they dismantled it, cleaned it and it was working again."

In June 1962, James returned to Hong Kong by plane. Paulette did not go with him because he had to tell his family that he had married a foreign girl. Paulette went to stay with a Spanish friend and her family in Valladolid until the end of July. Then she was told that James had informed his family that he had indeed married a foreign girl; they had more or less accepted it.

In late July, Paulette boarded in Naples the very same Italian "Asia" ship which had brought her husband to England so many years before.

It was full of "returning" students and stopped at Alexandria, Aden, Karachi, Bombay, Sri Lanka and Singapore. There were possibilities for sight-seeing and Paulette saw the Pyramids. Along the way, she also met members of the families of students and contacts she and her husband had met. It was an interesting trip.

Two Wives, Eighteen Children

In August, the ship finally arrived at the Ocean Terminal in Hong Kong. In those days, it was just a long wooden pier, with no building on it. In the middle of this terminal, Paulette could see a group of about 30 people. It was her husband and family waiting to greet her. Most of them were very curious but polite and welcoming enough. A traditional "Wedding Ceremony" took place five days later, Paulette was given a traditional gown to wear; she had to serve tea to her mother-in-law and aunts and was given a Chinese name by her father-in-law.

The culture shock was enormous. Paulette had never left Europe and spoke no Cantonese. But some of her brothers and sisters-in-law could speak English. She was joining an enormous and complicated family.

Her father-in-law had been an English-language interpreter with the Hong Kong Government. He had had two wives, including the present one. The first wife had died giving birth to the ninth child. He had nine more children with the second wife, who was younger than his elder daughter.

There were many tensions, aggravated by the fact that the 12th and 13th son had just "escaped" from the Mainland and returned to Hong Kong. During the Japanese occupation, Paulette's father-in-law had sent his four sons, then aged 13, 12, 11 and 10, together with his seventh daughter then aged 17, to the Mainland as a "safety measure" to live with a cousin.

But the cousin had moved away, the sister died of typhoid and the four young boys found themselves alone there. Paulette's husband

Paulette prepares flowers for the Chinese New Year.
(© Paulette Yvonne Octavie Lane)

and his brothers would never talk about the hardship they suffered; at the end of the war, the 10th and 11th sons (this one being Paulette's husband) had returned to Hong Kong, but the 12th and 13th stayed in the Mainland.

The 12th son had done well, was heading a large factory in Manchuria and had permission to come and visit his family. On the last visit, he had decided not to return to the Mainland. The 13th son was a doctor in south Mainland; he came via Macau by "snake-boat". All this had happened about six months before Paulette arrived; there was a lot of tension as the two returnees were not fitting in well.

The family lived in a large and confusing house in Bute Street in Mongkok. It had many short and long staircases and a garden on the roof where Father-in-law kept his collection of very prized Bonsai trees. The kitchen was on the second floor and the dining room on the first floor, two sons lived in the house with their families and had more or less separate quarters. Paulette struggled to remember the names of the siblings and their family numbers – "Who was who?"

Feeling the shock would be too much for her, her husband rented a small apartment on McDonnell Road. Some-in-laws never visited and, in fact, never accepted her. Some did come and helped her to adjust. "My father-in-law did not accept me initially. He was always exquisitely polite and would invite me for 'tiffin' (lunch) – just the two together – several times a week. He would comment – kindly – on the fact that I did not hold chopsticks properly – and that I had difficulty to adjust to the local customs. He wanted me to go back to France, although he did not say so directly. He ordered dishes that he knew I did not like or would find difficult to handle.

I wanted to be accepted, so I asked an old friend of my husband to teach me how to use chopsticks elegantly and teach me a little more about customs. I did not mention this to my husband as I did not want him to worry. On the day I felt confident enough, at lunch, I told my father-in-law I would not leave Hong Kong... he said nothing, but never invited me for "tiffin" again, but our relationship really improved. In the last years of his life, I became quite close to him and he even once said he was sorry he had not welcomed me with open arms."

Paulette's mother-in-law was different, and she immediately got on well with her. She was an uneducated woman and did not speak any English. Many children from the first marriage took advantage of her and burdened her with chores. "She gave me a gold necklace and I would accompany her to the local tailor where she took hours choosing 'cheongsams'. She had a wonderful smile which lit up all her face."

Paulette went to work as a secretary at the Chargeurs Réunis, a French shipping company, and then the Belgian Consulate as an assistant to the Commercial Attache. The work was interesting enough, but Paulette was restless.

Their first child, daughter Michele, was born on September 20, 1963 at the Hong Kong Sanatorium, "Father-in-law came to visit and gave me a small bottle with a green liquid that looked like Chartreuse. It was snake bile. It was quite bitter but he said very good for women who had just given birth. My mother-in-law brought hard boiled eggs, cooked for hours in a dark sauce with pig trotters and ginger roots. I swallowed it all because it was well meant, but it was hard just the same.

"My 14th sister-in-law had been waiting for me to give birth and to 'purify' for six weeks before her wedding." But, on that day, Paulette felt very ill with a kidney infection and had to be hospitalised. She lost seven kilos in the process. Paulette remembers that her mother-in-law spent much time with her and gave her many soups with strange herbs; she recovered well.

Their second child, son Eric, was born in September 1967. This was the year that the Chinese Cultural Revolution spilled over to Hong Kong. Many bombs were placed in lifts in hotels, public parks, bus and tramway stops; many people lost their lives when they were detonated. The headquarters of this campaign were in what is now the old China Building and the government response was directed from the Hilton Hotel, where the Cheung Kong Centre now is. There were numerous clashes with the Hong Kong Police. It finally died down when the movement died in the Mainland.

"Only British Can Be Lawyers"

Paulette had become restless work-wise; both her husband and father-in- law became aware of it.

"It was the idea of Father-in-law to enrol me in a newly introduced extra-mural law degree course. At that time, Hong Kong had no law faculty. This programme was initially meant for the many government servants who wanted this kind of degree.

"It was a three-year University of London Law Bachelor course. Several lecturers were provided by the university; local solicitors and barristers with special knowledge were also requested to give courses. It ran from 17:30 to 21:30 five days a week. The yearly exam was the same taken by students at the University of London. The course was popular, but demanding; several students abandoned it after the first month or two. So, when applications were made for the next three-year course, the application process was more accessible.

"My father-in-law went to enquire but the course was already full. So, my name was put on the waiting list."

Paulette remembers that, when her husband and father-in-law told her there was a vacancy and brought her the application form to be signed, the course had already started for more than a month.

"I absolutely lacked confidence to do a Bachelor Degree in English law. But those two were very persuasive and so I started thinking I would probably drop out after a month or so. But, to my surprise, I liked it very much and finished the entire three years."

In those days, it was not sufficient to have a law degree to be a lawyer. To become a solicitor, one had to do "Articles" – three years working as a trainee in a law firm. At that time, many firms charged a very hefty premium for taking in trainees.

Paulette trained as an articled clerk with Johnson Stokes & Master, a leading firm and one of the oldest law firms in Hong Kong. She did not need to pay a premium; but she received no salary, except for a gift of HK$200 and two Camembert cheeses at Christmas. After three years, she passed the qualifying exams and became a solicitor.

But there was a problem. Paulette was French and the rule then was that only British citizens could become solicitors. So she had to give up her French nationality and obtain British nationality through her marriage. Later, France changed its laws and so did the requirement for being British. But it took Paulette two years and a mountain of paper work for her to get her French nationality back.

She stayed for a further six years as a solicitor with Johnson Stokes

& Master. She asked about becoming a partner but was told that the firm was not considering women as partners – this of course changed later, but at that time this was the firm's policy. So, in 1976, she and three other solicitors founded the firm of Stevenson & Co., which later became Stevenson, Wong & Co..

In the 1970s, French clients were becoming more and more numerous. They liked to deal with someone who was a qualified solicitor and also spoke their language fluently. More French people are fluent in English these days, but then not many people could speak fluent French.

For many years, she advised and helped many French businesses who wanted to do business in Hong Kong; she created local structures, helping with leasing of offices, drafting contracts and obtaining visas. It was a great deal of work and required much explaining, in view of the different legal systems.

Selling the French Consulate

Paulette was active in the French community. The French Consul General's Residence in the Mid-levels proved to be the best overseas investment the French Government had ever made. It was originally the residence of the British Colonial Secretary. It had very beautiful European architecture and large grounds. The building was magnificent, with its columns giving it a touch of *Gone with the Wind*.

By the end of the 1970s, it had become too expensive to maintain. The then Consul General proposed selling it and giving part of the proceeds to the construction of the French School, a project close to his heart.

There was at that time no French School in Hong Kong; the nearby French lycees then were in Tokyo and in Phnom Penh. The idea of a French School was very much in the mind of business people who wanted their children educated in Hong Kong up to a high level. The government was very much in favour and was proposing free land,

In 2007, Paulette received La Legion d'Honneur from the French government. This photo was taken at the French consulate in Hong Kong. (© Paulette Yvonne Octavie Lane)

provided that an English stream was also provided.

The large banks and construction companies were all in favour. The French Consul General wanted a contribution of HK$5 million from the French Government. In 1983, the building was sold for HK$120 million, a record at the time.

The staff of Stevenson, Wong & Co. (© Paulette Yvonne Octavie Lane)

With this money, they bought a large villa on The Peak as the residence of the Consul-General, six apartments in Hong Kong and two entire floors for consular administrative offices at the Admiralty Centre with use of the roof. It was a very interesting deal. Paulette's firm handled the transaction; she also ensured that the HK$5 million needed to start the French School would also be provided out of the proceeds. Paulette drafted the first constitution document for the French School.

Since then, France has been owner of all its consular offices. Over the years, the apartments were sold and the consular residence on the Peak, a beautiful colonial building from the beginning of the century, was sold for HK$58 million.

In 1993, Paulette was one of five founding members of the French Mutual Assistance Fund (Fonds d'Entraide des Français de Hong

"I wanted to be accepted, so I asked an old friend of my husband to teach me how to use chopsticks elegantly and teach me a little more about customs."

Kong, FEF), a charity to help French citizens who find themselves in a difficult situation in Hong Kong.

The Fund took care of the last remaining French women, who had found themselves in Russia, had somehow later made their way to the Mainland and were living their last years in Hong Kong.

At the same time, there were also quite a few young people who had come to Hong Kong in search of work; many did not speak English and had no funds to return home. The Fund has continued to provide many people with assistance, ranging from a one-time loan of HK$1,500 up to urgent medical expenses for more than HK$140,000.

Retirement

In 1994, Paulette retired from Stevenson, Wong & Co. but continued to work for them as a consultant for a further six years. She then became consultant to Gicquel & Co., Bernadette. Bernadette was also a French citizen qualified as a solicitor and remained with her until the end of 2018.

From 1992, Paulette and her husband began to spend part of the year in a house they had bought in the southwest of France. He loved opera and classical music and, although he spoke practically no French, he was very close to the small community there. He died in 2004 of cancer. She had to decide whether to stay in France or return to Hong Kong. But her mind was made up when the French Government decided to build a motorway through the area. It expropriated the house and bulldozed it. She returned to Hong Kong.

19

Campaigner Against Global Tobacco Leads Fight from Hong Kong

Dr Judith Mackay

Dr Judith Mackay has lived in Hong Kong since 1967. Since 1984, she has been one of the world's leading campaigners for tobacco control.

"I realised that I could save more lives if I specialised in preventative, rather than curative medicine," she said.

"Currently, tobacco costs seven million deaths a year and losses of US$2 trillion in health care and lost productivity alone. This figure will rise to 10 million [deaths] by the year 2025. As the burden of this epidemic has shifted from rich to poor countries, most of my work is in low- and -middle-income countries in the Asia-Pacific region.

"The tobacco industry never stops. It uses all kinds of measures and products, including low-tar, filters and e-cigarettes. I have a job for life and will go on working until I am 100. I will never retire."

Since 1984, she has worked out of a room in her home on Clearwater Bay Road, with a spectacular view of the Clearwater Bay hills. She lives there with her husband John, a retired medical doctor. Her current position is advisor to the Global Centre for Good Governance in Tobacco Control (GGTC), based in Thailand. It has a global remit.

Childhood and Education

Judith Longstaff was born on July 18, 1943, in Saltburn-by-the Sea, a small village in Yorkshire on the northeast coast of England. It was World War Two. Her father was a captain in the British merchant navy, which he had joined in 1912 at the age of 15. He spent his whole life in the service and was away at sea for all but a few weeks each year.

Judith did not see him until she was almost two. In 1941, his ship was requisitioned and used as a troop carrier. His war service was very dangerous, with one ship torpedoed under him; it left him adrift at sea for 24 hours. Her mother was one of the first women in Britain to go to university. She encouraged her two daughters to study. An outstanding student, Judith passed her university entrance exams at the age of 16.

"I studied physics, chemistry and biology at A Level and decided to study medicine at university. It was a six-year course, followed by a one-year internship. My parents fully supported me, both psychologically and financially."

In 1960, she went to Edinburgh University, which at that time accepted a high percentage of women students – 36 of the 160 in her year. After graduating in 1966, she worked at the City Hospital in Edinburgh with Sir John Crofton, one of the earliest pioneers who linked tobacco with bad health.

In March 1967, after giving a presentation at the hospital on a complicated medical case, she met John Mackay, a Scottish doctor working in Hong Kong who had come back to take a post-graduate exam. "As soon as I saw him, I knew that he was the man I would marry."

After a whirlwind romance, they married in July 1967. He returned to his private practice at Drs Anderson & Partners in Hong Kong; she stayed in Edinburgh for three months to complete her internship at City Hospital, before joining him.

Learn Medical Cantonese

On arrival in Hong Kong, her first task was to learn colloquial and medical Cantonese, to enable her to work as a doctor. "I found this very difficult, but it was essential in enabling me to continue professional work."

She did part-time research with the Paediatric Department of the University of Hong Kong (HKU). Her two sons were born in 1969 and 1970. Then she spent three years in a training programme in internal medicine in the Medical Faculty at HKU. After passing many examinations, she obtained membership of the Royal College of Physicians of the United Kingdom.

In 1971, the couple made a momentous decision. They were living in a rented 3,000-square-foot apartment in St George's Court,

Kadoorie Avenue in Kowloon; one morning they received a demand from the landlord to increase the monthly rent by HK$100 for the next three years.

Deeming this unacceptable, they went house-hunting. That very day they found a bungalow in Clearwater Bay Road, built in 1957, with 2,500 square feet and a garden of one third of an acre. The price was HK$300,000. They decided to buy it, using all their savings, money from her parents and a limited mortgage from a bank.

It has proved to be the best investment of their lives; 50 years later, they are still living there. "It is the reason we are still in Hong Kong. Many expats live in subsidised apartments; when they retire, they cannot afford to stay on."

In 1972, Judith flew to the Philippines to select a couple to work for them. The Mackays built a 450-square-foot extension for them to live in. The wife worked as their amah and the husband looked after the garden, the swimming pool and their three guard dogs. They would work for the Mackays for 40 years. The next generation of the same Filipino family is working with the Mackays to this day.

From 1976 to 1984, Judith was deputy head of the Medical Department of the United Christian Hospital in Kwun Tong. Government figures showed that the largest preventable cause of death was tobacco smoking, over 3,000 a year.

"There was a maxim on the male medical ward that we 'never admitted a non-smoker'. Cancer, heart disease, stroke and chronic bronchitis – all tobacco-related – were our most common admissions. I came to feel my work was a patch-and-repair job. So many of these diseases were irreversible, even with expensive technology. I realised that the overall health of Hong Kong's population would never improve until there was an appropriate emphasis on prevention. I felt the urge to move into this field."

This determination was strengthened when she learnt that more women died from smoking than from all methods of birth control combined. "Cigarette ads promise emancipation, whereas in reality smoking is yet another form of bondage for women."

Fighting "Big Tobacco"

So, in 1984, she took the difficult decision to leave her senior
position at the United Christian Hospital (UCH) and dedicate herself
to the campaign against tobacco. A second reason was the need to
promote local Hong Kong people to high positions at the hospital.

"During the last three months, I had to tell my patients I was
leaving. Some burst into tears and begged me not to go. They asked
how I could leave them. It was the saddest thing." At UCH, the medical
Cantonese she had learnt was invaluable. "Without it, I could not have
done my job. A nurse was always there and could step in. But I was 90
per cent all right."

She swapped the bustling hospital for the silence of an office
room in her house. The change meant not only losing the company of
her patients and hospital colleagues but also no pay. "At first, it was a
lonely existence. Then support came from one cancer doctor in Hong
Kong, then governmental support from Geoffrey Barnes (then Deputy
Secretary for Health and Welfare). Tobacco control advocates from
around the world gradually made contact, and I, in turn, have managed
to establish networks throughout Asia."

This campaign meant taking on the giant global tobacco
companies.

Her work quickly became bitter and personal. The transnational
tobacco firms were rich and powerful and had the backing of
governments. They saw Asia as the most important future market, as
control measures began to cut consumption in the United States and
Europe.

They attacked her, the media and anyone else who said that there
was a link between smoking and disease. At public hearings in Hong
Kong in 1985 on whether to ban tobacco advertising, she was sitting in
the official area, with tobacco company executives; her teenage sons sat

In the 1980s, with her students at United Christian Hospital. (© Judith Mackay)

in the public gallery. "The boys heard the Philip Morris team discussing me personally and professionally in words such as the boys had never heard before (and which are unrepeatable)." The experience persuaded the two to be non-smokers for life.

The tobacco industry frequently threatened her with law suits. Smokers' rights groups compared her to Adolf Hitler and sent her death threats. In 1990, she learnt from a leaked, confidential document published in London that the transnational tobacco industry considered her "one of the three most dangerous people in the world" – a badge she wears with pride!

Her first victory came in 1986, when she persuaded the Hong Kong government to ban the import, manufacture and sale of smokeless tobacco products. The government came under intense pressure from US Senators, the commercial officer of the US consulate

World Health Organization

Department of Health

ld Health Organization Collaborating Cen
Cessation and Treatment of Tobacco De
Launching Ceremony
9 April 2012, Hong Kong

The launch ceremony of the World Health Organisation
Collaborating Centre for Smoking Cessation and Treatment of
Tobacco Dependence in Hong Kong. (© Judith Mackay)

and the tobacco companies. Nonetheless, it implemented the ban in early 1987, the first place in Asia and the second in the world to do so.

Later that year, the Hong Kong government became the first in Asia to establish and fund a tobacco control agency. It appointed Mackay as the first Executive Director of the Hong Kong Council on Smoking and Health (COSH). For the first time in three years, she had a salary. As a result of COSH's work, Hong Kong has now one of the lowest smoking rates in the world – 10.2 per cent of the population aged 15 and above in 2019. "Hong Kong has been a model for Asia. COSH is where I learnt to lobby and deal with governments."

In 1989, Judith meets Chinese Prime Minister Li Peng and his wife Zhu Lin. (© Judith Mackay)

Health Advisor to Many Countries in Asia

Mackay was overwhelmed with requests for help from neighbouring Asian countries. So, in 1989, she resigned from COSH to establish the Asian Consultancy on Tobacco Control, to share information, experience and expertise among countries in the Asia-Pacific countries.

At that time, 60-70 per cent of men and 2-10 per cent of women in Asia were smoking every day. The number was rising due to growing population and affluence, more smoking among girls and lack of funds for tobacco control. China alone had over 300 million smokers, more than the entire population of the United States.

Mackay has concentrated on this work for the last 32 years. "US and British tobacco companies have adopted double standards in low- and middle-income countries. They advertise in ways long banned on home turf, sell cigarettes with high tar and no health warnings. The trade arm of the US government threatened unilateral trade sanctions against countries that refused to open their markets to foreign cigarettes or curtail their marketing."

So, she criss-crossed the world, speaking at international conferences and testifying before government committees in exporting countries. She asked that tobacco companies follow the same standards in developing countries as they did in their home country and that a product as harmful as tobacco not be used as trade leverage.

"[US] Congressional hearings on tobacco were tense, with tobacco industry-funded Congressmen directing extreme aggression toward me."

In Asia, she became a health advisor to many countries, including China. She has helped them to draw up comprehensive tobacco control legislation, speak at conferences and workshops.

"My modus operandi has been to respect countries and work with them. I never tell governments what to do, as some western advisers do. Governments invite me to come and I offer my advice. I always look at the position of each government and see what is possible. I give support and documents.

"In 1990, I was the first non-Russian consultant to visit Mongolia. They were relieved that I was a woman. The night before I was due to leave, the Minister of Health came to see me and asked me to draft a law on tobacco control. I spent the night doing it and it was passed a year later."

The work took her all over Asia. In the last three months of 2019, before COVID-19 shut down the world, she visited 17 countries.

"After three to four years of support, Asian countries competently run their own tobacco control programs and national campaigns take on their own momentum. I inform and empower countries to get their national tobacco control efforts up and running."

Global Treaty

In the 1990s, she became a senior policy adviser to the World Health Organisation (WHO). She presented the concept of an international United Nations-style treaty on tobacco control. The negotiations took several years and the *Framework Convention on Tobacco Control* (WHO FCTC) entered into force in 2005.

This puts countries under an international legal obligation to implement measures in this sector. It has been ratified by 182 nations, making it one of the fastest track United Nations treaties in history.

This is what the convention website says: "The WHO FCTC was developed in response to the globalisation of the tobacco epidemic. The spread of the tobacco epidemic is facilitated through a variety of complex factors with cross-border effects, including trade liberalisation and direct foreign investment. Other factors such as global marketing, transnational tobacco advertising, promotion and sponsorship, and the international movement of contraband and counterfeit cigarettes have also contributed to the explosive increase in tobacco use."

Contributing to this treaty, with its global reach, is probably the most lasting achievement of Judith's professional life.

In 2002 and 2006, she published *The Tobacco Atlas*, sponsored by the WHO and published by Myriad Editions, and later by WHO or other health organisations. This, and a website tobaccoatlas.org, provide a comprehensive guide to the production and consumption of tobacco in the world. They outline obstacles to tobacco control, in particular the tactics of the tobacco industry, and what tobacco control

In 2007, Judith was named as one of the 100 Most Influential People in the World by *TIME* magazine. She is with her husband John Mackay. (© Judith Mackay)

measures governments should take. They are surprisingly similar around the world. *The Tobacco Atlas* also explains global smoking, second-hand smoking and its adverse health effects – co-morbidities, deaths and broader costs to society. Later editions were published by WHO and other health organisations.

In 2006, she was appointed Project Co-ordinator for the launch of the World Lung component of the Bloomberg Initiative to Reduce Tobacco Use in low and middle-income countries.

Judith has received many awards, including the USA Surgeon General's Medallion in 1989: the Silver Bauhinia Star from the Hong Kong government in 2006: an OBE from Queen Elizabeth in 2008: and a "Lifetime Achievement Award" from the British Medical Journal Group in 2009.

Family

Her two sons studied at Cambridge University. One became a doctor who lives in Edinburgh and the other an environmentalist living in Cambridge. She and her husband normally spend the summer holidays with them and their grandchildren.

She plays golf every Friday with her husband. She also enjoys swimming, walking in the Sai Kung countryside and relaxing in her garden. Since 2007, she has taken classes in Tai Chi, with her favourite two Tai Chi sword programmes.

"We have lived in Hong Kong for 54 years. It is my home and my love. We definitely plan to continue to live in Hong Kong."

"We have lived in Hong Kong for 54 years, this is my home. I love this place."

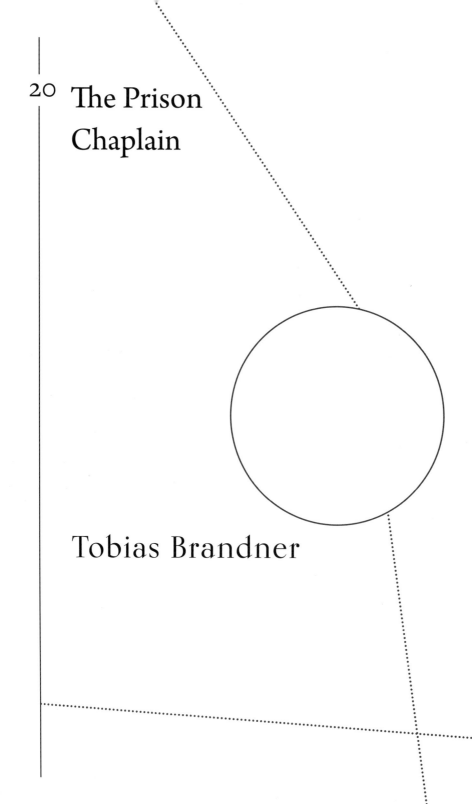

20 The Prison
Chaplain

Tobias Brandner

A resident of Hong Kong since 1996, Tobias Brandner is professor of theology at the Chinese University of Hong Kong (CUHK) and continues the mission of ministering to inmates of the city's prisons that he began on Christmas Day 1996. He is an ordained minister of the Swiss Reformed Church.

"I am most blessed. I am very passionate in what I do here," Brandner said.

He was born in 1965 in Auenstein, a farming village of 1,500 in the north of Switzerland. He was one of five children of a medical doctor. "Ours was a comfortable, middle-class family. Everyone knew everyone in the village and we helped our neighbours at harvest time."

As he was growing up, his parents encouraged his intellectual curiosity with books by Sigmund Freud and Erich Fromm and on Zen Buddhism. "At 15-16, I read these books and was very moved. It was like life was opening up. I decided to dedicate myself to the deepest quests – what is the meaning and purpose of life? I even considered going to a Buddhist monastery, in Japan, if not in Switzerland."

His parents were liberal Christians, going to church every week and sending Tobias to Sunday school. In the final years of his secondary school studies, he had the opportunity to study Hebrew.

"Our teacher was a wise elderly pastor who taught us with joy and brought us closer to theology. We should consider it with a critical mind. Theology is more practical than philosophy, which is purely speculative. It is something you must engage with and practice in life." For his university degree, he was torn between theology and medicine.

In 1984, he graduated from secondary school. It was Easter, a lovely time of the year. He was spending a week with the family of his girlfriend. "I felt that my life was before me; spring was full of life."

Then, on a Saturday morning, he received a telephone call from his family: his father had taken his own life on Good Friday, aged just 50. "It was completely unexpected. It was a result of depression. I had seen him tired and with a temper. At the morgue, I saw him, he was very peaceful. I had to confront the futility of life. Why are we here?

What do we do with our life?"

The tragedy made him change his plans. Instead of going to study in the French-speaking part of Switzerland, he chose the University of Zurich so that he could stay closer to his mother. It also helped him choose theology for his university degree. "It deals with the ultimate mysteries in life. I learnt that there are no answers. God is the answer, He is also a mystery. I learnt to deal with it."

One book that greatly influenced him was *Letters and Papers from Prison* by Dietrich Bonhoeffer. He was a German Lutheran pastor who publicly opposed the Nazi regime. The Gestapo arrested and imprisoned him in April 1943. He was executed in April 1945, allegedly for involvement in an assassination attempt against Adolf Hitler.

"As a testimony of someone politically engaged against a dictatorial government, the work contains deep thoughts from prison. It also convinced me that Christianity is compatible with a modern worldview." At the university, Brandner completed a B.Th., M.Th. and a Ph.D in theology.

He was ordained as a pastor in 1991. "There was no day of conversion. It was a very slow, gradual process, rather a process of gradual surrender. I was passionate about being engaged in society."

He worked one year in the church. Between 1991 and 1995, he served part-time as a minister in prisons. "I did it with passion. It was very meaningful."

In 1994, he was elected as a member of the city parliament of Zurich; he also did ecumenical work. In 1995, Brandner married his long-term sweetheart, who had just graduated as an interior product designer at an art school in Switzerland. For their honeymoon, they did a six-month bicycle tour of Africa, from Zurich to Cote d'Ivoire. They used Swiss-made bicycles, which they are still riding nearly 30 years later.

His wife said that she wanted to work outside Switzerland, perhaps somewhere else in Europe. Brandner wrote to the Basel

Mission, the country's most important Protestant foreign missionary organization, asking if they had an opening and expecting that he might find a position as a teacher in a theological school in Africa or Latin America. Three weeks later, a letter came from the Mission, saying that they were looking for a candidate for the prison ministry in Hong Kong.

"I was overjoyed and jumped in my apartment, embracing my flat mate. I immediately knew that's it. I had never been to Hong Kong, neither did I ask for a try out. There was no hesitation, no discussion. We immediately knew we would go."

He had no connection with the city. "Hong Kong is a great city. I realised that my wife could get a job there, which she would not be able to in rural Nigeria. I preferred it to Africa, where you are always the white and expected to give money. Both sides create the superiority complex. In Hong Kong, we are on an equal footing. My wife was equally positive."

The offer of the Mission was generous – salary for two years and payment of fees for full-time study of Cantonese for him and his wife at the Yale-China Chinese Language Centre at CUHK. They arrived in August 1996. "Cantonese is a great language, with so much wit in it. Hongkongers have such a great sense for jokes."

On Christmas Day 1996, he made his first visit to a prison at Shek Pik. From 1997, he started to spend half to a whole day a week in prisons, in one-on-one meetings with inmates. He started with English-speakers and then moved to Chinese prisoners with some English.

"I saw more and more Cantonese-speakers. They did not mind my limited Cantonese. They had time for me; there is no time pressure in prison. We met in the legal visiting room, with no officer present."

In the summer of 1998, he finished his language studies. In September that year, he started as a full-time prison visitor; he also began to work as a part-time professor at Chung Chi College at CUHK. In December, the government gave him a chaplain's pass; this allowed him to visit all the prisons in the city, to every part of them, with no limit of time and no staff present. He was the first minister to receive this pass who was neither Anglican nor Catholic. "People were very patient and gave me guidance. You must follow the rules – take nothing in or out nor contact family members on your own."

Brandner said that those in prison were not necessarily bad people. "They are just ordinary people in extraordinary circumstances. The prison system is a place that punishes and offers rehabilitation; however, there is little done for rehabilitation. I believe that faith plays a crucial role in changing not only behaviour but also a person's heart and mind. I love these guys. Of course, they have done wrong things, some of them seriously wrong, but I do have deep respect for them, as they cope with their captivity."

A prison chaplain is challenged to grasp what is most needed by the person he encounters. "You most easily establish relationships with outgoing ones, but they are not necessarily those who need it most. Finding a way to talk to the more introverted ones is important – I have to constantly remind myself to leave the comfort zone... What I aim is leading them on a path of growing ability to love and receive love. What I do, ultimately, is to communicate God's forgiveness."

He never tries to convert the inmates. "Faith is the experience of being accepted and loved despite all our broken-ness. I cannot convince you. You need to surrender to this deeper truth in life and that is why, theologically speaking, we call it a gift. It is not you who decide to be a Christian. It is really God's spirit which moves you. And this moving means receiving this amazing gift that you are accepted the way you are."

He worked as a full-time prison minister until 2007. Then he took a year's sabbatical, unpaid, in Koh Samui in Thailand, with his wife and three children, born in 1997, 1999 and 2002. During this year, his wife worked there. He wrote *Beyond the Walls of Separation* about Christian faith and ministry in prison; it was published in 2013.

His contract for Hong Kong had expired and he had to decide

Photo above – Tobias Brandner visiting inmates of prison. Below –
Speaking with prison inmates. (© Tobias Brandner)

"What I aim is leading them (the prisoners) on a path of growing ability to love and receive love."

Talking with students. (© Tobias Brandner)

his next move. Mission 21, the successor organization to the Basel Mission, encouraged him to apply for the post of Director of Mission, based in Basel, Switzerland. With much reluctance, he eventually did apply but, unexpectedly, was not chosen.

"For a few months, I was narcissistically hurt. But more and more, I realized that God saved me, as I had made a wrong decision to apply. As a result, in 2008, I came back to Hong Kong as a full-time professor, with part-time prison visits. I was very happy to return."

Brandner works in the Divinity School of Chung Chi College, Chinese University of Hong Kong. "We are the only theological school within a public university in Greater China or possibly even in Asia."

He teaches the history of western and Asian Christianity and Christian missions and researches the religion's shifting centre of gravity to the East. The department has around 200 students, with about 70 new entrants a year. About 15-20 graduates a year will become ministers; the others will join non-government organizations

Teaching students. (© Tobias Brandner)

or go on to doctorate studies. The courses include an M.A. in Christian Studies, which is not training for the ministry.

He continues prison visits one day a week. Once a month, he takes his theology students to Shek Pik Prison for joint worship. "They always love to go and find it rewarding. A lot of them become friends with the inmates."

During the COVID-19 pandemic, his wife and three children stayed in Switzerland. His wife runs a travel business running tours for foreign visitors coming to Hong Kong; during the pandemic it has been in hibernation.

"My three children have graduated from secondary school. They see Hong Kong as their home. My big mistake was not to buy an apartment in the late 1990s. I have always lived in accommodation provided by the mission or by the university. This makes it impossible to stay here after retirement. I plan to continue working here until I reach retirement age."

A life full of travel, good deeds, intellectual stimulation and multicultural influences. The young boy playing in the fields of Auenstein could not have imagined such a path.

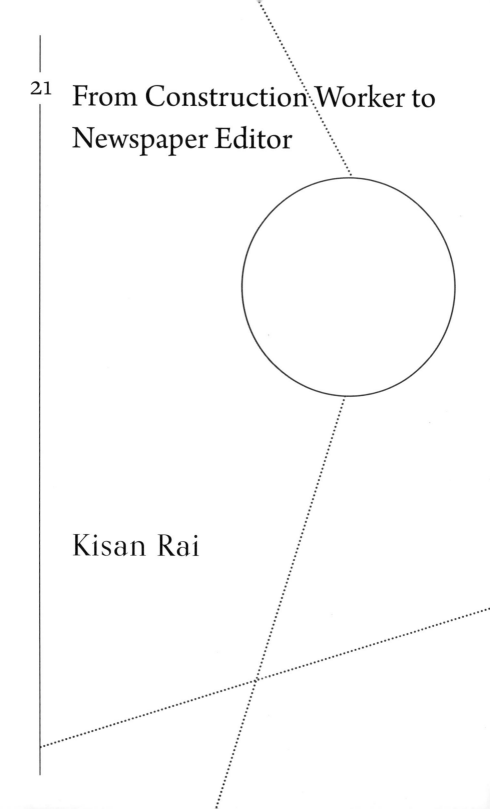

21

From Construction Worker to Newspaper Editor

Kisan Rai

When Kisan Rai arrived in Hong Kong, he shared a single room with his new wife and five members of her family. He had to wait eight months for an identity card before he was able to work – two years of toil and sweat on construction sites 300 foot above the ground.

Rai later became editor of *Everest Media*, the only Nepali-language newspaper that serves the 21,000 members of the community in Hong Kong. He earned a monthly salary of HK$20,000 and had a comfortable, if not easy, life. He was president of the Hong Kong branch of the Federation of Nepali Journalists.

"Before the handover, Nepalis were fearful that all would change. This has not happened. The governance here is still different to that in the Mainland. So, they feel more secure than before. Those who work in mainstream society can speak and understand Cantonese," Rai said in an interview in Hong Kong in May 2021.

The Nepali community includes rich and poor – chief executives of construction companies, many who own their own businesses, including bars, restaurants, jewellery shops, beauty salons and groceries, as well as those who work as manual labourers as Rai did.

"Before, people felt insecure here and invested in Nepal. Now it is the other way around. They sell their property there to buy here. When those in business retire, they will stay here and not go home," Rai said.

In 2020, Rai won an apartment in a lottery for the Home Ownership Scheme and bought a two-bedroom unit in Nam Cheong with 500 square feet for HK$4 million. He paid 10 per cent and has a 25-year mortgage; most will be paid back by his elder son, who plans to work in Hong Kong after graduating in computer programming from a university in Britain. It was his fourth attempt at the lottery.

Growing up – Bangalore and Nepal

A small flat in a Hong Kong tower block was a world away from Rai's early life.

He was born on October 7, 1967 in Bangalore, southern India. He and his sister were children of a soldier in the Indian army. In 1971, their father took early retirement and took his family to live in Dharan, a city of 170,000 people in southeast Nepal. His father bought land and became a farmer.

Rai attended primary and secondary school and college in Dharan. At college, he specialised in Nepali and social studies. "The country has over 100 ethnicities, each with their own mother tongue. My parents used their mother language. But at home we spoke Nepali."

It uses the same Devanagari script as Hindi. Many Nepalis are, like Indians, Hindu. The majority of Gurkhas were Buddhist or belonged to other religions specific to their ethnicity.

As a student, Rai joined one of Nepal's several Communist parties. But, after he moved to Hong Kong, he changed his view.

In 1992, after graduating, Rai founded a primary school in Dharan and became its principal. He rented land and erected a small wooden building with six rooms. He was joined in the project by his sister and brother-in-law. He served as principal for seven years.

"Initially, it was only a primary school. It is flourishing today, with 500 students at primary and secondary level," he said.

In 1994, he married his sweetheart, the daughter of a Gurkha soldier in the British Army. Since she had been born in Hong Kong, she had the right of permanent residence. She attended primary school in Hong Kong. In 1990, her father retired and moved back to Dharan, where she went to secondary school.

"It was a love marriage, inter-caste," Rai said. Nepalese are divided into ethnic groups, each with its own culture and originally from its own area. The Nepalese call their ethnic groups "jats". Conservative families only permit marriages within their own ethnic group. But the rules are breaking down in the cities, where young people often marry the partners of their own choice.

The couple decided to move to Hong Kong, where some of his wife's family lived. Rai handed over the post of school principal to a colleague. In 1998, they took the plane to what was for him another planet.

Homesick on the Construction Site

Arriving in Hong Kong was a complete shock. "It was totally different to my home city. I had never seen such tall buildings. In Nepal, nothing is higher than 10 storeys. Everywhere was crowded with people and the pace so fast. The food was different. It was very hard to adapt."

Their accommodation was also a shock. In Dharan, homes were spacious. But here their new home was a single room which the couple shared with five members of his wife's family; they had no privacy.

His wife worked and lived six days a week in a nursing home for old people, for which she earned HK$5,500 a month; it was arduous and stressful. He was on his own those six days. But he could not work because he did not have an identity card; this took eight months to obtain. Her salary was barely enough for them to live on.

"During that time, I was homesick. I thought of going home. But no, I thought, I am here, I must do something."

After obtaining his ID card, he went to work on a construction site. He started with a cleaning job for three months in Tin Shui Wai for HK$300 a day. That at least was on the ground floor. The next assignment was on a 30-storey government building in Sham Shui Po.

For a school principal who had never been higher than 10 storeys, it was intimidating. "It was so high up. I was afraid. The job lasted four months." Next was even worse – a 40-storey structure in Ma On Shan. One day I did not know how to operate the machine I was on. I was 30 floors up, about 300 feet. I pressed the wrong switches and fell five storeys. I was very scared. Fortunately, I had a safety harness." He earned HK$15,000 a month.

His fellow workers were Chinese and Nepali. They spoke to each other in Cantonese. Sometime his Chinese colleagues mocked them: "'Do you have trains in your country? Do you have planes?' they asked. They thought our country was so backward. My Cantonese is still not good. I sometimes have a problem when I go shopping."

The next post was on the construction of the MTR in Mei Foo. "I was very bored. I remember walking in the rain the whole day. I missed my home."

He was desperate to find an escape from this back-breaking work and approached six fellow members of his community; they agreed to publish the SAR's first daily newspaper in the Nepali language for the 17,000 compatriots living in Hong Kong. Together they put up HK$80,000 and set up Everest Media Limited. They produced the first edition on May 1, International Labour Day, in 2000. Finally, Rai could put away his hard hat and safety harness.

Raising Money

The project did not start well. After three months, they had run out of money and the company faced closure. Rai told his partners he could save it. He went to see Tej Bahadur Rai, a wealthy Nepali, chief executive of Sunkoshi Construction Limited. He told him that media was very important to their community; if he could help, Rai could make it work.

Fortunately, his namesake stepped forward with a loan of HK$100,000. He then became a partner in the company and provided a further HK$200,000. They did not have to pay back the money.

They spent HK$270,000 on a second-hand computerised printing machine made in Heidelberg, Germany in 1965. They printed 1,000 copies a day, with 12 pages; the price was HK$4, sold through grocery shops in Yuen Long, Jordan, Yau Ma Tei and Tsim Sha Tsui.

Most of the editorial work was done by 10 full-time editorial staff in Kathmandu, the Nepali capital, who e-mailed the stories to Hong Kong. Rai added local items, including activities in the community and news translated from English media, like the *South China Morning Post*, *The Standard* and Radio Television Hong Kong. It also carried advertisements.

"The paper is for the Nepalis in Hong Kong to read about what is happening in Nepal and also to strive for unity among Nepalis here," said Rai. He operated out of a small office on the second floor of a commercial building in the centre of Yuen Long.

After 18 months, the paper became a weekly, then a bi-monthly and, in 2019, a monthly magazine in paper and online. They publish 2,000 copies a month; it is free. Rai earned a monthly salary of HK$20,000. The operation did not make a profit. The magazine showed the need of the community to stay in touch with what is happening at home. There is constant coming and going between Hong Kong and Nepal.

Missing His Sons' Childhood

Rai's wife earned more than he did. After he started working on the construction sites, she became a saleswoman at Stanley Market. She trained as a beautician and opened her own business next door to the office of her husband. Their income was steady and life became easier.

The couple have two sons, who were 18 and 25 years old in 2021. The parents saw little of them. The elder one was born in Nepal and remained there after his mother returned to Hong Kong. He was brought up by Rai's mother and sister and received his education in Nepal.

For university, he went to London where he took a B.A. in computer programming. By then, Rai's sister and her husband had emigrated to Britain, where they looked after him.

The second son was born in Hong Kong but also spent much of his life in Nepal, where he attended primary school. For secondary school, he returned to Hong Kong and aimed to go to Britain for college.

So, Rai was an absentee father for most of the life of his sons. "We used to see them once every three years when we visited Nepal," he said. "We speak all the time via WhatsApp. I feel close to them." This was one price he and his wife had to pay for living on such modest means in Hong Kong; they could not afford to educate their sons there.

His wife has visited the sons once in Britain. Rai planned to go with her in 2020; but the COVID-19 pandemic made it impossible. He never went to Britain. His elder son planned to move to Hong Kong and live with his parents after his graduation.

This suddenly became easier in 2020, when Rai won an apartment in Nam Cheung under the Home Ownership Scheme. It was his fourth participation in the lottery. The cost was HK$4 million for a two-room unit with 500 square feet; he paid 10 per cent down and signed a 25-year mortgage.

Most of the money will be paid by his son. Rai and his wife planned to retire to Dharan when he reached 60. They purchased a house there. "Life will be easier for us there. But my son has more opportunities in his field here," Rai said.

Life Improves for Nepalis

The Nepali community here is a legacy of the Gurkha Brigade of the British Army which served in Hong Kong. Most are children and grandchildren of Gurkha soldiers and their families who decided to stay on. Before the handover, the Gurkha soldiers left Hong Kong. There are 3,000 serving in the British Army. Since 2008, those Gurkhas

"The paper is for the Nepalis in Hong Kong
to read about what is happening in Nepal and
also to strive for unity among Nepalis here."

(© Online Khabar)

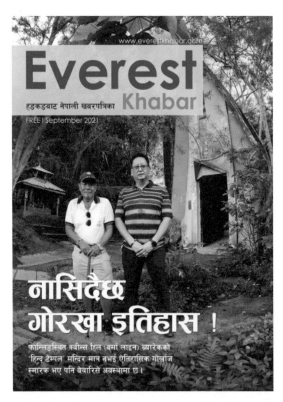

On the magazine cover:

www.everestkhabar.com

Everest
हङकङबाट नेपाली खबरपत्रिका **Khabar**

FREE | September 2021

नासिदैछ
गोरखा इतिहास !

फान्लिङस्थित क्वीन्स हिल (बर्मा लाइन) ब्यारेकको
'हिन्दु टेम्पल' मन्दिर मात्र नभई ऐतिहासिक गोर्खाज
स्मारक भए पनि बेवारिसे अवस्थामा छ ।

This issue of *Everest Khabar* was the last Kisan Rai published
before his passing. (© Everest Khabar Facebook Page)

who retired before 1997 have had the right to settle in Britain.

Rai said that, before the handover in 1997, Nepalis did not feel sure of their future after Chinese rule. "We thought that all would change. But this has not happened. We do not feel insecure. While Hong Kong is part of China, its governance remains different to that of the Mainland."

The community includes: wealthy entrepreneurs who own construction companies; proprietors of more than 100 grocery and jewellery shops and beauty shops; workers on construction sites and in the security industry; and owners of two dozen bars and restaurants, some in Soho and Lan Kwai Fong. "These were started by people who went to work in the food and beverage industry and then set up their own businesses."

The historic weakness of the community has been their inability to read and write Chinese. Before 1997, they lived in military cantonments and had little contact with the local population. This inability has blocked them from many jobs. Rai said that most Nepali children studied in English-medium schools but that those who work in mainstream society, especially in retail and dealing with a largely Chinese clientele, spoke and understood Cantonese.

This growth had made people more secure in Hong Kong. "Those in business will retire here and not go back to Nepal. Before, they bought property at home. Now they are selling those properties and investing the money in property here."

Law and order in Hong Kong is very good. "Violence is frequent within our community, but not from Chinese," Rai said.

A majority have Nepali passports, some have British ones and a few SAR passports, for which they must surrender their Nepali nationality. The majority find their marriage partners within the community: only a few marry Chinese or Westerners.

"At home, Hindu culture is very narrow and parents find it hard to accept children marrying outside the community. But, in Hong Kong, people are more open-minded. Many are not Hindu, they are Buddhist and Kiratist (the religion of the ethnic Kirati people of Nepal, Sikkim and Darjeeling)."

Rai felt that in Hong Kong Nepalis can freely celebrate their religion and traditional festivals – with the limitation that public holidays are few, so that they cannot celebrate so exuberantly as at home.

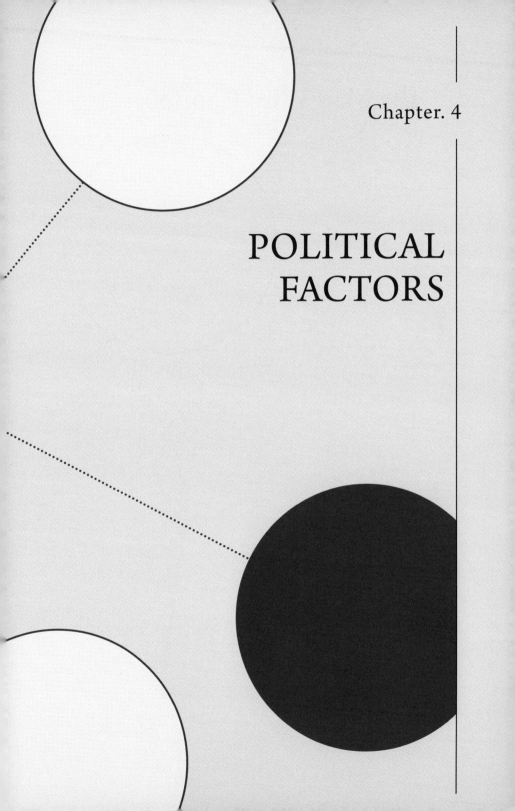

Chapter. 4

POLITICAL
FACTORS

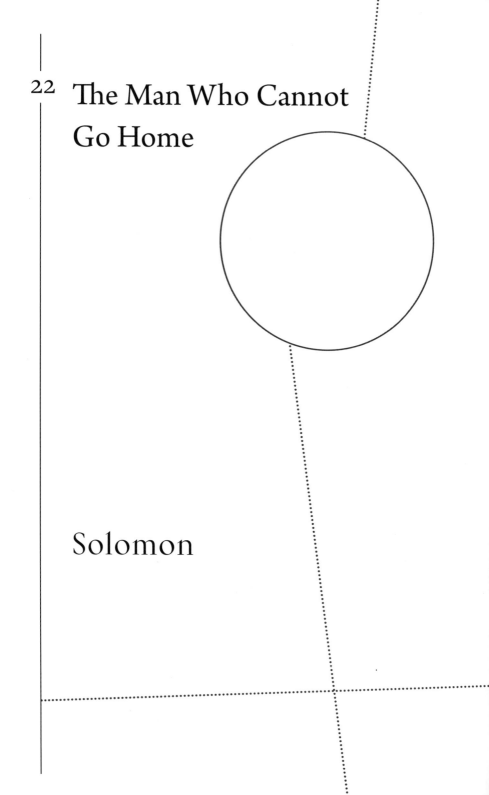

22

The Man Who Cannot Go Home

Solomon

It was four o'clock in the afternoon on June 26, 2004 when Solomon received the telephone call that changed his life. "The secret police is assigned to deal with you," a friend said. "You must leave Burundi at once."

Friends and members of his church drove him at once to the city's international airport from where he boarded a plane. He was carrying nothing, not even a small bag. He thought he was going to Australia but found that he had arrived in Hong Kong. "I knew nothing about it, except that it was in China, and that I did not need a visa to enter," said Solomon.

For 17 years (as of 2021), Solomon has been living here, waiting for the day when he can return home and live again with his wife and five children. He talks to them every day via WhatsApp. "I hope for a change of regime at home which would permit my return. The chance of that is about 40 per cent. God can do everything. My faith is essential to me. It is what keeps me alive."

Solomon is not his real name; he asked that it not be used, in order to protect his family from possible reprisals by the government. He has been granted international protection and is able work after a long court case.

The Immigration Department detained him for five days before releasing him. "Everything was arranged by his church members back home. The United Nations knew where I was."

This status makes him different to nearly all the 13,000 foreigners here seeking political asylum. Only the 243 who have been granted asylum are allowed to work. The rest are not permitted to work; while their applications are being processed, they live on a modest subsidy from the government and charities.

In 1964, Solomon was born into a privileged family in Bujumbura, the former capital of Burundi. His father was an officer in the army. He was the eldest of nine children; the family lived in a spacious house, with servants looking after them. He went to the city's best schools, where he excelled as a student. At 16, he joined the national basketball team.

"My parents were very proud of me. They wanted me to become a soldier or a priest. We were devout Catholics and went to Mass every Sunday. I attended a seminary which trained young men to become priests. I had a very good teacher who had studied in France. My mother was a civil servant."

But the road to priesthood was blocked by his father's demand that, as the eldest son, he must marry and have children to carry on the family line. At university, he studied law; on graduation, he joined the civil service as a lawyer.

A landlocked country in East Africa, Burundi has 11.9 million people living on 27,834 square kilometres of land; it is one of the smallest countries in Africa. It has had a tragic history. From the 17th century, it was an independent kingdom. In 1894, Germany conquered the area and turned it, with the neighbouring country of Rwanda, into a colony. After its defeat in World War One in 1919, Germany ceded the colony to Belgium, which governed it until independence in July 1962.

The population is 84 per cent Hutu and 15 per cent Tutsi. During the colonial period, the Belgians favoured the Tutsis, giving them preference in education and government jobs. Since 1962, the country has experienced two civil wars and genocides, coups d'etat and political instability. More than 80 per cent of the population lives on subsistence agriculture.

Solomon said that the main source of conflict was the difference between Tutsi and Hutu. He himself is a Tutsi. "This conflict was largely man-made. We all have the same language and the same religion (the country is over 90 per cent Christian). The myth was created that the Tutsis were 'foreigners who invaded from the north.'"

According to a study by the United Nations Population Fund and the Burundian government, 116,000 people were killed between October 21 and December 31, 1993. These included both Tutsis and Hutus and followed the assassination of President Melchior Ndadaye

Bujumbura is one of the two capitals of Burundi. (© iStockphoto)

on October 21 during a coup attempt.

"Of the deaths, 90 per cent were Tutsi," said Solomon. "This was the mass killing of people for no reason. Entire villages were wiped out. It was the first genocide in Africa."

Solomon worked as a government lawyer for six years. He married his sweetheart; they had four sons and one daughter. He had a comfortable life. Then, in 1994, aged 30, he made an important decision – to leave the government and work as a human rights lawyer.

"I was inspired by Steve Biko, the human rights activist in South Africa who campaigned against apartheid. He believed in equality between people, that you should not be against another person because of their religion or their colour."

In 1973, the South African government placed Biko under a banning order; he was frequently detained. After his arrest in August 1977, state security officers beat him to death; he was 30. Over 20,000 people attended his funeral.

In Burundi, Solomon worked as a lawyer for the League of Human Rights. He enjoyed a certain privilege. Some of his associates had been imprisoned and tortured and left the country, but he was able to visit detention houses and see the inmates.

"I campaigned for change. Some people in the government gave me information." But then came the call on the evening of June 26, 2004 and his sudden departure to Hong Kong.

After the Immigration Department here released him, those looking after him sent him to a dormitory where other people were also staying. He was in a state of shock. Nothing had prepared him to stay in this city on the other side of the world, with which Burundi had no connection. He left behind his wife, then pregnant, and his five children. "It was an emergency. If I had gone to a European country, I would have needed a visa." But there was no time to apply for one.

During his early months in Hong Kong, NGOs (non-governmental organisations) assisted him. They found him a place to live, which he shared with others, and paid him pocket money each month. "It was just after the SARS epidemic. Everyone kept their distance."

After he settled down, he went to work for Christian Action, to help those seeking political asylum. It was established in 1985 as a registered charitable organisation, to serve the disadvantaged, marginalised, displaced and abandoned and give them hope, dignity and self-reliance. Solomon worked there for 15 years.

In February 2021, he moved to the Justice Centre in Sai Wan, where he has continued the same work. Founded in 2007, the Justice Centre is a NGO which works to provide fundamental rights and access to justice for the most marginalised in society. These include: asylum seekers; refugees; and victims of torture human trafficking and forced labour.

Hong Kong has about 13,000 political refugees; they seek asylum or protection based on claims of torture and other mis-treatment in

Founded in 1985, Christian Action aims to help the weak in society. (© Christian Action)

their home countries. They have lived here for between a few months and more than 10 years. About half come from South Asia, 30 per cent from Southeast Asia and the rest from Africa and South America. The government has granted political asylum to 243.

Each year the government spends about HK$1 billion to handle asylum claims. Since 2013, those who have received asylum have been allowed to work and can send their children to government schools.

Historically, Hong Kong has not been a place of asylum, except to ethnic Chinese. The Immigration Department view is that Hong Kong has a "long-established policy of not granting asylum and we do not admit individuals seeking refugee status." The approval rate of claims of torture is less than one per cent, compared to 25-50 per cent in developed countries. This makes the work of Solomon and his colleagues very difficult.

In an effort to reduce the number of asylum seekers, the government has proposed some reforms in its Immigration (Amendment) Bill 2020. It would increase the penalty for those illegally employing refugees and allow the detention of someone whom the police believed to pose or be likely to pose a security threat to the community; currently, detention is only possible if someone breaks the law or is awaiting deportation.

Another reform is to introduce the Advance Passenger Information System (API System). This would require airlines to provide passenger and crew member information to the Hong Kong Immigration Department before departure; and the department could order the removal of those whom it did not want to admit to the city.

Towards Hong Kong, Solomon has mixed feelings. "I am full of gratitude that it gave me refuge. I am in total security here. I recognise that." But he has always felt out of place. "People here have a culture completely different to mine. The society is closed and inward-looking. People are not open to foreigners. That includes refugees, domestic helpers and even mainland Chinese. They know nothing but their own affairs. I do not wish to stay here, but I have no choice."

Like many Africans in China, he has had to endure insults and stupid questions. "People ask me if we have rice and motor vehicles in Africa. When others are buying skin cream during the summer, the person in the shop asked me why I don't need one, I replied that it is because I have black skin, I don't need it to protect myself against sunburn and skin cancer. These people know nothing.

"Once I was playing basketball with a young boy. He went to his father and said that I was ugly. His father slapped him. But I said to his father: 'It is you who have taught him. You are responsible. People fear Africans. Students need to be taught that the only difference between them and us is our skin colour."

But he has never suffered violence or theft of money. "Chinese prefer to trick you or lie to you, rather than steal from you."

He lives in a modest apartment in the New Territories for which he pays HK$3,800 a month. Has he considered relocating his family to another country in Africa or elsewhere? "This is not a decision I can make myself. I am in the hands of the United Nations High Commissioner for Refugees. They must be satisfied that I would be safe in another country."

Every day, through WhatsApp, he speaks to his wife and five children; during his absence, they have all grown up. His wife has come to Hong Kong to see him twice, his children once, in 2019. "When I left, they were very small and understood nothing. My family was supported by friends and the League of Human Rights. Life has been very difficult for them. The father is the head of the family. I remain very close to them." His Christian faith is very important to him. "It keeps me alive. I have not lost hope of a change in my home country that would allow me to go home. I rate the possibility at 40 per cent. I would take the first flight."

23

Turkish Kurd Stranded in Hong Kong, Will Retire Here

Mesut Temel

Mesut Temel is a Turkish Kurd who was born in 1972. After seven years of study and work in Taiwan area and the Mainland, he settled in Hong Kong in 2006. Since then, he has lived here with his wife and three children and works for a company that trades computer and telecom components.

Now he cannot leave the city. While the Hong Kong government in 2017 approved his application for a Naturalisation as Chinese, the Turkish consulate did not complete the process of renouncing his Turkish nationality. Without this, the Immigration Department will not act. So, since 2020, he and his wife have no passport and are stateless; they cannot travel.

"The consulate does not say what crime I have committed. Originally, I planned to retire in Turkey and bought an apartment in Istanbul. As things are, we will retire in Hong Kong. I am fine with that. I am a Hong Kong person."

Born in the Cradle of Civilisation

He was born in 1972 in Mardin, in southeast Turkey. It is an ancient city with more than 3,300 years of history and with a population of different races, including Arabs, Kurds and Arameans. He was one of eight children, six boys and two girls, of a poor Kurdish family. In 1977, his father took the family to Istanbul, the country's largest and most prosperous city.

The father did not want his children to grow up amid the conflict between the Kurds and the Turkish government. In 1982, Mesut's father was killed in a car accident. Mesut was one of the two fortunate children in that he was able to study chemical engineering at Middle East Technical University in Ankara, a course taught in English.

A friend of the family was doing business in Taiwan area and invited him to go there. "Like most Turks, I did not know where Taiwan area was on the map. My family told me to go for two years and agreed to cover the fees. Our family has a strong bond. Everyone lives

Temel and his family in Istanbul in 1978. (© Mesut Temel)

in the same building, with different apartments for each family."

He arrived in Taiwan on April 22, 1995. "I did not know where I was. All the signs were in Chinese. I realised I must study Chinese. When I went to the Taipei mosque for prayers, I found that most did not speak English."

A visit that was meant to last two years ended up lasting seven. He enrolled at the Language Centre of China Culture University in Taipei; he studied there for two hours each morning before going to work in the company of the family friend, an electrical engineer, who traded electronic goods.

He was such a good student that the university gave him a scholarship. At the mosque, he studied the Quran and taught it to children; he met many people there. He particularly liked the writings of Muhammad Fethullah Gulen, a Turkish Islamic scholar born in 1941 and founder of the Hizmet (Service) movement; it has three-to-six million members around the world. It had schools, foundations and other institutions across Turkey.

"What I liked about his work was that it rejected the clash of civilisations," said Mesut. "It said the opposite and promoted the interaction between different faiths and cultures."

In Taipei, he and Turkish friends founded the Istanbul Club as a cultural centre. They invited Taiwan friends and introduced them to Istanbul and other cities and aspects of Turkish life and culture. Once a year they invited 40 Taiwanese to a two-week bus tour of Turkey; they arranged for them to stay with local people in different cities and have direct contact with them. "They had a rich experience. Some wept on the plane flight back to Taiwan. When I married in Istanbul in 2003, 26 Taiwan people attended my wedding."

Love out of Earthquakes

Two devastating earthquakes in 1999 brought Turkey and Taiwan area even closer together. The first, on August 17, was the Izmit earthquake, measuring 7.6 on the Richter scale, in northwest Turkey. It killed more than 17,000 people and left more than 250,000 homeless. A massive international rescue effort was launched, with teams arriving from many countries in Europe and the Middle East.

One Istanbul resident who thought his house would collapse was Faisal Hu Guang-zhong, a Taiwanese and member of the Buddhist Tzu Chi Foundation, who felt the quake more than 60 miles away from Izmit. Sad that no-one had come from Taiwan area to help in the rescue work, Hu wrote an article in the *Min Sheng Bao* newspaper in Taiwan area. Master Cheng Yen the leader of Tzu Chi, read the article and was moved. She instructed her volunteers, then in Kosovo on a charity mission, to go to Turkey and report how Tzu Chi could help.

"When I saw the pictures on television, I wept," said Mesut. "Hu asked me to go to Turkey to help."

Tzu Chi started a fund-raising campaign in Taiwan area and sent a team to Turkey to deliver tents and build new homes. Mesut went with the team and acted as an interpreter.

Then, a month later, on September 21, the southwest region of Taiwan area was hit by the Morakot earthquake, which killed more than 2,400. It was one of the worst earthquakes in the history of the island.

To help in the rescue work, Turkey sent a team of government officials and volunteers. Mesut accompanied them in their work. He was also active in auctions and other money-raising activities in Taipei, Chiayi and other cities.

Move to Hong Kong

In 2000, Mesut paid his first trip to the Mainland, visiting Guangzhou, Shanghai, Beijing, Xi'an and Tianjin. "It was a very special feeling," he said. It was an era where many Taiwan companies were moving their production to the Mainland. He took the opportunity to visit suppliers and clients. He spent half a year in Guangzhou, working with a partner. Then he spent most of one year living and doing business in the United States. "Things did not work out well with my partner. I did not like the environment there."

In July 12, 2003, he married his wife in Istanbul. She is, like him, a Kurd, from Diyarbakir, in southeast Turkey. It is a city of 1.7 million, many of them Kurds. After the Treaty of Sèvres in 1920 following World War One, many Kurds saw the city as the capital of an independent Kurdistan. But this did not happen.

"It was an arranged marriage in the traditional way," Mesut said. "I met her several times before the wedding and had to ask for the acceptance of her parents. Her father was a retired Imam. She never lived in Taiwan area. She wanted someone rich not in money but in the heart."

The first test for the new couple came in Shanghai with his new wife being served Chinese food. Most Turkish people hesitate to taste Chinese food at first. But she ate a great deal, including durian (a fruit with a distinctive, strong odour). "She is a traditional woman, but open to new cuisines."

Their first child was born in 2005. In 2006, the new family moved to Hong Kong and rented an apartment in Tseung Kwan O. Two years before, Mesut had set up his company whose main merchandise line was flash memory products.

The move to Hong Kong was a shock. "I did not know many people, except Turks. People here did not speak Putonghua and our apartment was small. I found the people colder and less friendly than those in Taiwan. The pressure of daily life is heavier. It was hard to make friends. But the culture here, in Taiwan area and the Mainland, is similar."

As he had in Taiwan area, he established with Turkish friends a cultural centre. Each person paid a sum and they rented premises for one year for the Anatolia Cultural & Dialogue Centre. Each week they hosted one or two activities, with lectures by professors and other guests and artistic events.

It was particularly active during the holy month of Ramadan, with activities on 25 days. "Part of Ramadan is to share with others. So we had events and exchanges with peoples from different communities. We invited them to dine with us when we broke the fast after the setting of the sun. The media stress conflict and prejudice. But, face to face, it is the opposite. We found commonality, we prayed together and discovered much in common in our different faiths. Hong Kong is a multi-cultural city. I have very good memories of those events."

In 2019, the centre closed down, because of economic reasons and pressure from the Turkish consulate.

His company provides him with a steady income. "I have been in this sector for a long time and built up a network of contacts. I pay a great deal of attention to trust and honesty. In religion, cheating others

Photo above – Temel in Taiwan in 1996. Below – Temel at the Great Wall in 2000. (© Mesut Temel)

is a major sin. So we have clients who have worked with us over a long period. Perhaps they have to pay a little bit extra, but they are willing to do so, to maintain the relationship."

Victim of the "Coup"

Mesut is one of hundreds of thousands of victims of a fake attempted coup d'etat on July 15, 2016 in Turkey. Units of the armed forces attempted to seize control of places in Ankara, Istanbul and other cities; from the air; they bombed government buildings, including the Parliament and the Presidential Palace. During the coup attempt, more than 300 people were killed and 2,100 injured. But forces loyal to the government defeated the coup attempt.

Following this, the government arrested tens of thousands of people, including soldiers and judges, and dismissed from their jobs thousands of civil servants and teachers. It said that the coup leaders were linked to Fethullah Gulen, who lives in exile in Pennsylvania in the United States. It designated him a "terrorist" and has, since then, arrested tens of thousands of people whom it says are linked to him and his Hizmet organisation.

Since the coup attempt, it has closed all Hizmet's schools, foundations and other entities in Turkey. The consulate in Hong Kong has designated Mesut as a supporter of Gulen and refused to process his application to renounce his Turkish nationality or to extend his Turkish passport.

Years have passed since the July 15 incident, and Turkish authorities have failed to produce any credible evidence linking Mr. Gulen to the attempt.

Yet, instead of investigating the truth, holding the real perpetrators responsible and bringing greater safety and security to Turkey, the government of President Recep Tayyip Erdoğan has used Mr. Gulen as a scapegoat, offering fabricated, politically motivated charges that smear his reputation and everything the Hizmet movement stands

Photo above – With the staff of the Mosaic
Centre. Below – Temel at the Mosaic Centre.
(© Mesut Temel)

for – peace, interfaith dialogue, tolerance and education. Mr. Gulen has repeatedly and vociferously denied any involvement in the July 15 events.

In Turkey, President Erdogan continues to brutalise his own people through purges, mass arrests and a wide-ranging crackdown on free speech and freedom of the press. He has drawn condemnation from world leaders and human rights activists across the globe for seizing nearly 1,000 companies and US$11 billion worth of private assets, arresting more than 55,400 people and shutting down 149 media outlets. Some 150,000 state employees have been dismissed and more than 260 journalists are currently imprisoned, making Turkey the world's leading jailer of journalists.

The government made it clear that the arrests have nothing to do with involvement in the July 15 attempt, but instead are conducted on the basis of guilt by association with the Hizmet movement. Women and children are the hardest hit among the victims, as the authorities do not refrain from arresting pregnant women and bringing them back to the prison after they give birth. Some 16,000 women and more than 500 children are jailed. Physical abuse, torture and rape in Turkish prisons have been reported and condemned by independent watchdogs such as Amnesty International, Human Rights Watch and United Nations' Special Rapporteur on Torture.

"In 2017, I applied for Chinese naturalisation and the Hong Kong government approved the application," said Mesut. "A condition for this is to give up my Turkish nationality. But the consulate will not do the paper work. Without it, the Hong Kong government will not give me a passport or even a travel document, to enable me to leave the SAR.

"The governments of Japan and South Korea have given passports to Turkish people in the same situation. I have written to the Commissioner of Immigration. I have gone with my lawyer to the Department, with all the papers, but to no avail. My passport and that of my wife expired in 2020."

"We found commonality, we prayed
together and discovered much in
common in our different faiths.
Hong Kong is a multi-cultural city."

This de facto statelessness has devastated the family. Mesut cannot go to the Mainland, Taiwan area or anywhere else to visit suppliers and clients and inspect new products. He cannot visit his large family in Turkey, to whom he is very close. He has to communicate with his elderly mother via Facetime or WhatsApp. His three children have Turkish passports but cannot travel with their parents.

Polyglot Childhood

Mesut's three children, all boys, have had a very unusual childhood. They are aged 8, 12 and 16; they have spent all their lives outside Turkey. Two are attending an international primary school in Tsuen Wan, Rosebud Primary School, with classes in English; it costs HK$8,000 per student per month.

The eldest is attending Delia Memorial School (Hip Wo) in Kwun Tong, also an English-medium school. "I speak Kurdish with my wife and Turkish with the children," said Mesut. "The eldest understands some Kurdish, but not the others. We have no books in Kurdish. My children understand Turkish but speak English among themselves. That is the language of their school and YouTube. The youngest knows some Cantonese. He takes eight hours of Mandarin in class at school. For university, they will probably go abroad. We do not know if we have enough money to cover the fees."

His exclusion from his home country has turned the future of the family upside down. "I bought an apartment in Istanbul, using the name of my wife. That is where we were planning to retire. For this reason, I did not buy an apartment in Hong Kong, which I regret now. So, we have to rent."

His children have Turkish passports which allow them to go home, but he fears they might be used as hostages against him and his family.

In his office, he works with his colleague. "He has a passport and can travel, to see clients and suppliers. I plan to pass my company to him. Then I will devote myself to cultural exchanges and volunteer work in Hong Kong."

A devout Muslim, Mesut is active in the United Muslim Association of Hong Kong. Founded in the 1980s, it is a registered charity and Islamic organisation that manages mosques, schools, and elderly care homes for the Muslim community in Hong Kong. Mesut works on the fund-raising committee and as a volunteer. His Arabic allows him to read, recite and understand the *Quran* but not to use in daily conversation.

24

Sleeping on Park Benches, Analyst at Goldman Sachs

Innocent Mutanga

After Innocent Mutanga arrived in Hong Kong from Zimbabwe in 2013, he spent four months sleeping on park benches and getting food by making orders for people at McDonald's. Now he works as an analyst for Goldman Sachs, one of the world's biggest investment banks.

His eight years in the city is a story of intense study and determination to overcome the multiple obstacles thrown in the path of people who are poor and black. Many are scarcely able to overcome them.

Home with No Toilet

Innocent was born on February 26, 1991 in Hwange, a mining town in the west of Zimbabwe. He was one of three children of a miner; the family lived in a house owned by the mining company. Since it did not have a toilet, everyone had to go to a nearby public bathhouse to wash themselves and their clothes.

"My father worked underground. There were shifts, one starting at 06:00 until 14:00. Later he became a policeman in the mine, wearing shorts as the colonial policemen used to do. I was aware that the coal dust was affecting his lungs," he said.

The one luxury in the house was a refrigerator. It enabled his mother to run a business selling fish. She went to Binga, a town next to a lake, bought fish wholesale and then stored it in the refrigerator and sold it to her customers. Neighbours also used it to store meat.

The health of Innocent's father deteriorated because of the coal dust. He died in 2000, aged just 38. The family lost the house and moved back to the rural area of Gokwe where his mother had grown up.

Innocent started school in Hwange and was an excellent student. He had to go to a new school in the rural area and found it a step down. "My first class was outside under a tree. We wrote in the dust. When the wind came, it blew our words away."

Language was another challenge. In the rural area, the teachers used Shona, the local language, and English. He had to learn Shona. In Hwange, he had spoken Nambya and Ndebele.

He stayed at the rural school for six years, before moving back to Hwange for secondary school; he lived in the house of an uncle. His favourite subjects were mathematics, physics and chemistry. His uncle switched off the lights at 21:00; Innocent opened the curtains to bring the light from large street lamps – enabling him to read for a further three to four hours.

"Almost everyone in the town went into the coalmines. Everyone knew I was different. They thought I would go into politics. My nickname was 'Desmond Tutu'. They still call me that today."

Tutu was the first black Bishop of Johannesburg and of Cape Town. He was an Anglican cleric and theologian, well-known for his work as an activist for human rights and against apartheid.

For his A Levels, Innocent went to Thornhill School in Gweru, capital of Midlands Province. His mother went to work as a domestic maid in the neighbouring country of Botswana, to earn money to pay his school fees.

He obtained an A in his four subjects – mathematics, physics, chemistry and further mathematics – and graduated in 2010. He earned a scholarship to Drake University in Des Moines, Iowa. "I liked the curriculum and the fact that it had many Asian students. I saw the future of the world as Asia."

But it was only a partial scholarship, so he had to raise money to cover part of the cost. He chose an unusual route – he contacted Zimbabwe's celebrities, politicians and footballers to ask for support. He went to the Reserve Bank, asking for a grant in exchange for a promise to work there after graduation. "I did not raise money, but I learnt a lot and met many of the important people in the country."

Finally, he started a chicken business to earn money. He also worked at the United States embassy in Harare.

"I was Able to Understand the US Beyond the Brand"

In December 2011, he flew to the US to begin studies at Drake in the spring semester. His major was actuarial science. He found the calculus class too easy but enjoyed the other subjects.

"The teachers were too nice. I am still in touch with two of them. As I hoped, there were many Asian students, mostly from Malaysia and one mainland Chinese who was my closest friend.

"In arts and social science, I wrote a paper on Malcolm X. It was a very good learning experience. I was able to understand the United States beyond the brand."

To earn money, he cooked fried chicken and chicken wings in the local Sodexo fast food shop. For exercise, he went jogging in the evening through the towns neighbouring Des Moines. "I found that police cars were following me. I thought they were protecting me. Then friends told me residents had called the police when they saw a black on the streets. I learnt of the danger of being a black in the U.S. Near the campus, the police had killed a black person."

Back into the Inferno

In July 2013, Zimbabwe was holding presidential and parliamentary elections. Thousands of people hoped it would be the moment to unseat President Robert Mugabe. He had been in power since independence in 1980 and driven the country into bankruptcy and international isolation.

Innocent decided to return home in December 2012 to take part in the election, principally to help people to register to vote. The election roll revealed an estimated one million invalid voters, including many who were dead, and excluded up to one million living ones. He planned to return to Drake after the election.

"My role was to help people vote. If the government suspected you of involvement with the Movement for Democratic Change (the main opposition party), you would be arrested at once. I was questioned by police as to whether I was working for the Americans or the French. I was also kidnapped by the secret police for a few hours and left unconscious."

By late January 2013, he decided that it was too dangerous to stay. On January 20, he went to Botswana, where he stayed for a few hours, and then went to South Africa. He chose a white town, Stilfontein, in North West Province. He started to teach work and was hired by the Lofdal Christian School in the neighbouring town of Klerksdorp.

In the election in Zimbabwe held on July 31, Mugabe was re-elected with 61 per cent of the vote; his party won 160 of the 210 directly-elected seats in the national parliament.

At the school, Innocent taught maths, physics and chemistry. He was so popular that the government hired him to teach at other schools, even providing a car and a driver. He even appeared on local television.

"I was too successful and attracted too much attention. One day two intelligence agents from Zimbabwe came to the school. I saw CCTV and recognised them. Fortunately, I was not at the school at that time. Many Zimbabweans in South Africa have been killed by such agents; the cause has never been established. I realised I had to leave at once. Twenty-four hours were too long."

The school's lady principal was sympathetic. She told her son to drive Innocent in his sports car to Johannesburg Airport. He took just two suitcases, one of books and one of clothes. From the car, he texted the airport sales office: what flights were available that day to a destination where a Zimbabwean citizen did not need a visa to enter?

The lady gave him the choice of an African country or Hong Kong, via Qatar. He knew nothing about it, other than it was part of China and English was spoken there. Of the two, he chose Hong Kong. Since he had only 200 rand (HK$200) in his pocket, the son of the principal paid the cost of the ticket – HK$11,000; he swiped nonchalantly his credit card through the machine.

Arrival in Hong Kong

"Once I was in the plane, I knew that I would be fine and that this was how it was supposed to be," he said.

After a long journey via Qatar, Innocent found himself in Hong Kong, a city of which he knew nothing and where he knew no-one. While he had the right to enter, the immigration officers were suspicious and ushered him into a small room.

Did he have enough money? In his pocket were only 200 rand (HK$200) and credit cards. "The cards had no money in them but I showed them to the officer. She nodded." She asked him where he planned to stay.

"I had no idea but she supplied the answer 'Chungking Mansions'." After 20 minutes, she allowed him to leave. Initially, Innocent thought a hotel with such a high-sounding name would be too expensive, but a Chinese lady he met that day explained that it would be most suitable, so he went there. An Indian rented him a tiny room for three days in exchange for the HK$200 he had in his pocket.

Since he had no money, the first four months were very difficult. For food, he waited inside one of four branches of McDonald's and persuaded people that he could get them a better deal if he ordered for them. He had studied the menus and worked out how to maximise the value of an order.

In this way, they had the meal they came for and he was able to squeeze extra money to buy something for myself. "I asked inter-racial couples as they were more likely to agree. I did not try couples that were both Chinese."

He slept in parks in the Kowloon area for four months. "I was often moved on, but, on one bench in Austin Road, I could sleep all night without being disturbed."

His visa expired after three months. He went to the city office of the United Nations High Commissioner for Refugees (UNHCR) which filed his application for refugee status. Once this application had been made, he had a legal right to stay in Hong Kong.

Gradually, he secured work – painting walls, teaching English to children recently arrived from the Mainland and editing college application essays for students. In Chungking Mansions, he met Professor Gordon Mathews, chairman of the Department of Anthropology at the Chinese University of Hong Kong (CUHK), and his students. He joined their discussions and asked the professor if he could attend his classes; he agreed.

"I took eight courses at CUHK. Other professors allowed me to attend their classes. I did not pay. I always did all the course reading, which most students did not. I always had something to contribute." From 2014, he spent five years at CUHK. "It was a long struggle. I had to re-take A Level exams, in sociology, psychology, mathematics and further mathematics."

Finally, in 2016, he was officially admitted as a student, one semester at a time. "Each semester I had to prove myself and was allowed to stay for the next one. Since I had to pay, I had to raise funds on my own. In 2019, I graduated with a degree in anthropology." He was the first refugee in Hong Kong, in 2017, to receive a student visa and the first to obtain a university degree. He considered working for a Ph.D in anthropology.

He was active outside the classroom, joining the CUHK English Debating Team and co-founding "The Wandering Voice", an online platform where domestic helpers, refugees and ethnic minorities could tell their stories.

In 2017, Goldman Sachs (GS) organised a business case competition, which is where competitors are given details of a business deal and asked to write how they would handle it. Someone urged Innocent to take part and said that he should go into finance; the man was one of several he approached in his efforts to raise fees for his studies. Innocent followed the advice. Most of the participants were finance and business majors; entry into GS was a plum job.

Innocent won the competition and joined GS as a summer analyst

Johannesburg Airport, from where Innocent Mutanga came to Hong Kong. (© iStockphoto)

from June to August 2018. He worked on equity trading (swaps), cross asset financing (trading and structuring) and other products. He received a monthly salary of HK$55,000.

Then, in November 2018, he joined the Silverhorn Group for three months as an investment trainee, doing investment/industry research and support clients. Silverhorn is a finance investment boutique founded in Hong Kong in 2010 with a focus on Asia.

In August 2019, Innocent joined the global markets division of GS as an analyst in its global markets division. He receives an annual salary of over HK$1 million. He lives in a rented apartment in Tian Shui Wai, for which he pays HK$11,000 a month. He talks regularly to his mother and brothers in Zimbabwe on WhatsApp.

He hopes to be in Hong Kong for a long time. "There are many opportunities here. I started with nothing and now have a chance to have something. What I have gone through has made me what I am – more resilient and more determined.

"Hong Kong is the top financial centre for Asia, ahead of Tokyo and Singapore. It has a good regulatory system. If you work hard, you

"There are many opportunities here. I started with nothing and now have a chance to have something. What I have gone through has made me what I am – more resilient and more determined." (© LinkedIn)

The Africa Center of Hong Kong goes to schools and rebrands the image of Africans. (© Africa Center of Hong Kong Facebook Page)

get results. For me, it is Asia's World City. In my network, I meet a wide diversity of people. But many people, especially locals, are not part of it. They see it from afar, like a parallel universe."

Innocent is a rare success story among the city's 13,000 political refugees. "Unfortunately, many charities tell them that they are victims. They do not realise their potential and exercise their competitive advantage. You should not fall into that trap."

Africa Center

In 2019, he founded the Africa Center Hong Kong in Tsim Sha Tsui. It is on the 12th floor of a commercial building in Hillwood Road. On its website, it says: "It is a platform and creative hub dedicated to rebranding how people think and feel about blackness or Africa by challenging and changing the narrative.

"The status quo is that blackness is seen as dangerous and/or vulnerable, two views that are racist and problematic. We work to challenge these perceptions. We work to achieve our goals through a number of workshops and events, which range from educational, food and arts programmes, such as African Literature Book Club, African cooking workshops and African dancing workshops. We have African dinner meet-ups and networking events," it said.

It publishes a monthly magazine *African Spear* (*Amplify Africa*), of which Innocent is co-editor. In the second issue, he wrote: "With the shift in global order, where Asia is becoming more significant geopolitically, economically and culturally, I realised that it was of paramount importance that we take ownership of our stories in this region.

"My moment of awakening came when I was reading Chinua Achebe's *Things Fall Apart*. This great historical fiction truly embodies my favourite African proverb that Achebe would echo as 'until the lions have their own historians, the history of the hunt will always glorify the hunter.'"

WHY FOREIGNERS LIKE HONG KONG

Author   Mark O'Neill
Editor   Donal Scully
Designer   Vincent Yiu

Published by Joint Publishing (H.K.) Co., Ltd.
20/F., North Point Industrial Building, 499 King's Road,
North Point, Hong Kong

Printed by Power Digital Printing Co. Ltd.
Unit A, 4/F., 45 Kut Shing Street, Chai Wan, Hong Kong

Distributed by SUP Publishing Logistics (HK) Ltd.
16/F., 220-248 Texaco Road, Tsuen Wan, N.T., Hong Kong

First Published in March 2023
ISBN 978-962-04-5152-2

三聯書店   JPBooks.Plus
http://jointpublishing.com   http://jpbooks.plus